My First Hundred Years
in Show Business

My First Hundred Years in Show Business

Mary Louise Wilson

The Overlook Press
New York, NY

This edition first published in hardcover in the United States in 2015 by
The Overlook Press, Peter Mayer Publishers, Inc.

141 Wooster Street
New York, NY 10012
www.overlookpress.com

For bulk and special sales, please contact sales@overlookny.com,
or write us at the address above.

Library of Congress Cataloging-in-Publication Data

Wilson, Mary Louise.
My first hundred years in show business : a memoir / Mary Louise Wilson.
pages cm
1. Wilson, Mary Louise. 2. Actors—United States—Biography. I. Title.
PN2287.W4925A3 2015   792.02'8092—dc23 [B]   2015010788

Book design and type formatting by Bernard Schleifer
Manufactured in the United States of America
ISBN: 978-1-4683-1085-6

First Edition
1 3 5 7 9 10 8 6 4 2

To my friend and guide,
Dennis

My First Hundred Years
in Show Business

I was swimming around in Edwina's pool having such a nice, refreshing time, when she said "You know, Diana, your future's behind you." "Your future's behind you!" I nearly DROWNED!

—Diana Vreeland, D.V.

1989

I WAS SITTING AROUND A TABLE WITH THE REST OF THE CAST ON THE first day of rehearsals for *Macbeth* at the Public Theater when the director rose from his chair, turned to me, and said, "First Witch? I'm giving your chestnut speech to the younger, prettier witch." Now, I wasn't crazy about playing this witch; let's face it, it's a generic crone role! But I hadn't worked on the New York stage in a long time.

For the past few years the only parts I was getting called to read for were washroom attendants and bag ladies on television. I was even going up for parts against actual bag ladies. I had gone from featured roles on Broadway to playing parts labeled "Woman" with lines like "Hello." So now I was telling myself well at least I'm *first* witch. Then this director took away the one thing that made me first: the chestnut speech.

I was shocked. I thought the best thing about performing a dead playwright's work was that your lines couldn't be cut. A director could make me wear a hat that covered my face or a farthingale that wouldn't fit through doors, but nobody was going to fiddle with my words. Especially not Shakespeare's. Not that I had a clue what the chestnut speech was about, but it had lovely, tongue-rolling phrases like "aroint thee" and

9

"rump-fed runyon" and "mounched and mounched and mounched." And now this guy was stripping me of my epaulettes in front of the whole damned company. To make matters worse, the witch he gave it to really was young and pretty, so he was not only rewriting Shakespeare, he was having a cheap laugh on me. This wasn't a career I was having, it was an exercise in humiliation.

How the hell did I end up here? I felt it was my fault, that I had caused or allowed it to happen. At the same time, I certainly didn't feel like I belonged down here.

There's an old refrain about the five stages of an actor's life:

1. Who is Mary Louise Wilson?
2. Get me Mary Louise Wilson.
3. Get me a Mary Louise Wilson type.
4. Get me a young Mary Louise Wilson.
5. Who is Mary Louise Wilson?

I was somewhere between stages four and five. I was dimly conscious of my own culpability, but at the same time I bristled at being taken for, *mis*taken for, a modest talent only suitable for maid parts.

You have to have a dream of something, you know, if you're going out to buy a pair of bedroom slippers, you have a dream of what you want . . .

F OR A FEW MONTHS NOW, MY FRIEND MARK HAMPTON—NOT THE deceased decorator, but the very funny and very much alive writer Mark Hampton—and I had been fooling around with the idea of writing a play about a woman named Diana Vreeland. She had been a powerful magazine editor and well-known figure in New York social circles for decades. Now Mark had become fascinated by recent newspaper accounts of her being blind and bedridden, her once jet-black hair turned white, and her jewelry and other personal effects being auctioned off at Sotheby's. We were both touched by her sad fate. I picked up her book, *D.V.*, a collection of her reminiscences and pronounce-ments as edited by George Plimpton, and reread it. I had read it years earlier, when it was given to me by a pal, Nicky Martin. At that time I simply thought it was wonderfully silly. We took turns reading passages aloud and keeling over laughing. This time, though, I fell in love with her unique use of language.

Just for kicks, I sat in a chair across from Mark and read a couple of her stories aloud. We looked at each other. This was great stuff. We knew it. We talked about the possibilities and the difficulties of writing about somebody still living. Mark had already been to hell and back writing a musical about the Boswell Sisters while one of them was still alive. Besides, I doubted we could get permission. Then one morning we came across her obituary in the *Times*. August 23, 1989. It hit me then that if we didn't make a move, somebody else was going to get their hands on that book and I would regret it for the rest of my life. So now, sitting stewing in the rehearsal hall, it occurred to me that I had nothing left to lose. On the first break, I went to the pay phone and called a lawyer I knew about get-ting the rights to *D.V.* I was going to write a play based on this book, and I was going to perform it in broom closets, if necessary.

*I*N THEATRICAL CIRCLES, MENTIONING THE NAME "MACBETH" IS believed to bring on extremely bad luck. If an actor utters it or any line from the play inside a theater, he or she must perform a ritual. There are variations of this ritual, but the one I know is to spit three times as you turn around three times in the dressing room doorway. It is conse-quently always referred to as "the Scottish play." Directors of the Scot-tish play seem to me to get hung up on the witches. The witches are their big, if not only, chance to exercise their directorial style. I've seen or heard of the witches appearing as pretty fairies, giant puppets, or male goth rockers. They can be played as real or they can be supernatural. Our director informed us that we were real, and that we lived off the refuse of the battlefield. In other words, we were bag ladies.

Maybe Richard felt bad about taking away my chestnut speech, because the second week he gave me a tumbrel. The idea was that I would lug Banquo around in it. This tumbrel looked like something out of *The Flintstones*. It had big clunky wheels and on its trial run down the aisle it got stuck. It was built too wide. I saw the set designer slap his hand over his face. After that I just lugged Banquo on and off upstage left. I can't remember now where I was lugging him to, or why.

A week after my first call to the lawyer, he called back; our quest for *D.V.* was hopeless. The famous agent Swifty Lazar claimed "planetary rights." My heart sank. Who would give me the rights anyway? Me, a fiftyish, thoroughly demoralized, demoted first witch? I didn't have the standing. The awards. Not to mention the shoes.

Something was definitely amiss in the Public Theater's prop department. We witches were told we would have bloody animal parts and entrails for the "boil and bubble" scene. What we got were little sticks with feathers glued to them, and our entrails were surgical hoses that bounced unconvincingly. Our cauldron was the size of an ashtray with a sliver of dry ice inside that refused to boil or bubble during our incantations. It waited until our backs were turned to burp a trickle of smoke, like a rebuke for being yelled at. The audience giggled.

The lawyer called again; apparently Swifty had been speaking allegorically. The rights to *D.V.* were in the hands of the Vreeland family. Their lawyer was George Dwight. We called Mr. Dwight and he invited us up to his office. He was very cordial, a gentleman of the old school. He seemed intrigued by the idea of a play about Vreeland, perhaps sensing money to be made, but we would need the approval of her sons, Tim and Frederick. He said he would contact them. Things seemed possible now. Mark and I went down the street to an expensive Italian restaurant and ate an enormous lunch.

*I*N THE SECOND WEEK OF PREVIEWS, A DESPERATE, SWEATY RICHARD suddenly decided that the witches controlled the weather. Confusion among the witch ranks: we thought we were real people. Nevertheless. He gave us instruments: a little drum for Second Witch, a triangle for Third, and a recorder for me. We reminded me of a kindergarten band. Three little witches from school. We were supposed to summon wind, thunder, and lightning with our instruments, but the sound and light cues consistently came too early or too late, causing more giggles from the preview audience.

> *. . . and as I can never find a pair of bedroom slippers I can get into, I've only got the dream. Not the slippers.* —*D.V*

*G*EORGE DWIGHT CALLED. THE SONS WERE INTERESTED, BUT A grandson, Alexander, objected to the idea of his grandmother being portrayed onstage. It was a fact that drag queens were "doing" her everywhere, and he feared, quite rightly, that we would make her an object of camp. So, down, down I went, "like glistering Phaeton, into the base court."

*T*HE NIGHT BEFORE THE LAST PREVIEW, RICHARD, HAIR ASKEW, wild-eyed, said to me, "You know what I want." I was very much afraid I did. "You want me to appear in the sleepwalking scene as the witch," I said. "Right," he replied.

I had been going along with the tradition of doubling as Lady in Waiting in the sleepwalking scene. Nightly, I traded my rags for a gown and a wimple. But now he wanted the hag standing behind Mrs. M. while she bemoaned her fate. "Give me one good reason!" I snapped. "Well," he thought for a minute, "the Macbeths are having a servant problem." I went to Lady M's dressing room and told her what he wanted me to do. She was a young thing, fresh out of Juilliard, possibly dating Richard. She didn't see a problem. "But it will steal focus!" I shouted. Shrug, no worries.

My actor buddy and occasional personal analyst John Seidman was staying with me at the time. I consulted him the next morning over coffee as I lay in bed and he sat alongside me in his briefs. I wanted to call Actor's Equity, but John advised going along with it. "He won't keep it in," he said. He was right. When I appeared that night in my foul rags, audience heads swiveling from Lady M back to me created a susurrus that nearly blew her candle out.

Give 'em what they never knew they wanted. —D.V.

*B*UT I DIDN'T GIVE A DAMN WHAT HAPPENED ONSTAGE NOW, BECAUSE Dwight had just called back again: the sons had decided to ignore the grandson's objections he said, they were in favor of a play about their mother. Oh joy! And then he said "Frederick Vreeland, 'Freckie,' wants to meet Mary Louise." Oh, God! This had not occurred to me. Of course he would want to see what I looked like! How could I possibly pass muster? How could I ever convince him I could play his mother? This woman dominated the fashion world for three decades. What to wear? What to wear? That persistent cry. This was the eighties and my uniform was hip-hugger jeans and turtlenecks. I no longer had a blueprint for myself in a dress. I ended up buying something in a mall—a noncommittal black linen sack and a pair of excruciating black leather pumps—and when I got it all on, combined with a pair of black stockings, I looked like somebody's Sicilian mama.

It was a boiling hot June day. The vestibule just outside the apartment door was lacquered red, and on the wall hung a painting of young Diana in a dress with a floating white collar. I stood there in my widow's weeds, stockinged legs itching, feet aching in my hard leather heels. I was back in dancing school, standing against the wall in a velvet dress that didn't fit, my precipitate breasts squashed under the bodice, my size-eight Mary Janes looming below me.

I rang the bell. Freckie greeted me wearing tennis whites, shorts, and a polo shirt. He didn't give my wardrobe a glance. He was gracious and easy. He took me to lunch around the corner. He was funny like his mother, and he chatted freely about her. He said she was not a very good mother—she was not around and had no sense about money—but when I told him that I revered her, he looked surprised and pleased. He told me that even when she was ill and bedridden, she continued having dinner parties. The maid would serve and the guests would talk to her through her closed bedroom door. Freckie's comment was, "Mom never liked to appear unless she was at full gallop."

After a few agonizing days, Dwight called to say I had passed inspection. Mark and I went to his office to sign the contracts giving us exclusive rights to *D.V.* Oh joy, oh rapture! We floated out of the office and down the street to another expensive restaurant and ate another gigantic lunch.

Some eras I've known are as dead as mud. But they were so great. —D.V

1940s

I MAY HAVE BEEN BITTEN BY THE VREELAND BUG AT A VERY EARLY age. Growing up in New Orleans in the forties, I was fascinated by the women my mother invited to our house to play bridge: elegantly dressed ladies with their little hats, their bright red lips and nails, their husky voices and phlegmy smokers' coughs. The way the metal clasps on their purses clicked open and closed importantly, their lipsticked cigarettes smashed in the ashtrays. Looking back, I realized that their drawls had the same touch of Brooklynese that Vreeland had. They weren't necessarily pretty; one or two of them looked like wizened little monkeys, but chic little monkeys, with diamonds in their ears. And they were often funny. I was an untidy child, big for my age with scabby knees and exploding hair, yet I longed to be like these women, to be glamorous and funny.

We moved to New Orleans from Connecticut when I was seven. My mother found and renovated an old house in the Garden District: white columned facade, high ceilings, marble fireplaces, and living room windows that went right to the floor. The rooms were beautifully furnished. My mother had a genuine talent for decorating. She had to have the best and the latest of everything. I think we had the first automatic dishwasher in the city; when turned on, it "walked" across the kitchen floor, scaring the hell out of the cook. But this house was to be my mother's dream fulfilled, the stage for her career as a New Orleans society hostess. Where the money came from to pay for all of it, none of us would ever know. When I looked at the mountain of bills cascading off her desk, I could feel the anxiety flowing out of it. It may be that some people were never paid. My father had been hired as an associate of the esteemed Ochsner Clinic, but he was a tuberculosis doctor, the "poor man's disease." I'm sure his salary was modest.

My father was handsome and charismatic. I was madly in love with him, but he stayed aloof behind his newspaper while our mother tyrannized us. My mother's mother was an Anglophile who worshipped the King of England and the little princesses, Elizabeth and Margaret Rose, who called the Queen "Mummy." Consequently, our mother instructed us to call her "Mummy." My brother used to say, "Mummy is the root of all evil." To us, she was a regular Hitler giving out endless orders and rules about manners: "Sit up," "Sit down," "Curtsy," "Say 'Sir' and 'Ma'am.'" Even now, in my eighties, I start to stand up when an adult enters the room. My mother taught us when sitting down at the dinner table to unfold our napkins and put them in our laps. I somehow missed the order about what to do with it when dinner was over, and to this day when leaving the table my napkin slides to the floor and I trip over it.

Mummy's father was a distinguished Presbyterian minister, and she saw herself as descended from royalty. She was obsessed with social rank. She wasn't ever where she thought she ought to be in the hierarchy, and her unhappiness was a black cloud over the family. Her feelings were forever getting hurt and her tears were a constant oppression. There was nothing we could do to stop the flow. It trickled down on us and divided us, and made us cruel. My father teased my mother until she cried, my older brother and sister teased me until I cried, and I teased the dog until she bit me.

The one thing that kept us all from killing each other was humor. We shared a highly developed sense of the ridiculous. My father was a champion scoffer, and he could not refrain from teasing our mother for her pretensions. We not only had a cook (in those days most Southern middle-class families had cooks), but also a butler. Family dinners got fancier and fancier, with linen napkins, candelabra, salad plates, salad forks, and finger bowls. When he got a load of the finger bowls, my father twitted, "What's this for, dear? For germs? I washed before I came to the table. What? What?"

Watching our father tease our mother thrilled us children. One night she started to say, "When I was abroad—" when he interrupted "You were a broad, dear?" We became hysterical. She had her moments. One night after some hectoring, the butler entered with dessert and placed it in front of her: molded grape Jell-O on a crystal plate. She rose from her chair, stood for a moment staring dreamily down at the quivering mound and then she slapped it. She slapped it so hard she broke the crystal plate and to our utter delight bits of Jell-O shot all over the table. Some even hit the wallpaper. She wailed, "I always wanted to do that!"

Another time the family was spending a Fourth of July weekend at a fishing camp and while Mummy was visiting the outhouse, my brother threw a lit firecracker onto the tin roof. There was a terrific explosion followed by dead silence and then Mummy stepped out. With great dignity she murmured, "it must've been something I et."

My mother inherited her timing from her minister father, who incidentally was an actor until he realized he would never get leading roles because he was short and his head was too big. He went into the pulpit instead and thrilled his congregation by reading from the Bible in a roaring baritone, tears pouring down his cheeks. He could be very funny at his own dinner table, and his grandchildren inherited his timing—a blessing from the grave. It's innate; you either got it, or you ain't, and we got it.

My brother and sister were both very funny people. Hugh was four years older than me, and Taffy was five. I longed to be accepted by them, but they weren't having any of that. We had a costume trunk in the attic. Didn't every family? In there were World War I puttees, top hats, ancient evening gowns, tailcoats, and fur pieces. It was family tradition to "dress up" on party occasions. One night, Hugh in an old tailcoat and Taffy in a tea gown danced a wild tango around the living room to a recording of "Jealousy," and my stern father laughed so hard tears ran down his face. I tried to join in, but was roundly rejected. I was only funny when I didn't mean to be. The sight of me wearing my dress inside out or my shoes on the wrong feet or coming home from kindergarten inexplicably covered in green paint made my siblings roar.

I don't recall ever being taken seriously. Tears were "crocodile tears," and temper tantrums—usually the result of being ignored—meant being sent to my room. To solitary.

When we were little, Hugh was constantly trying to kill me off. We spent summers in Connecticut with a bunch of cousins, and we used to play in an old boathouse down by the lake. It had a big upper room once used for Sunday bible meetings. Down below, there were rowboats rotting in the muck. One day, Hugh made up a game called "Heaven and Hell." The upper room was Heaven, the muck was Hell, and he was God. If you did what God told you to do, you got to go to Heaven and run relay races, and if you didn't, you went to Hell in the muck. I was five and Hugh was nine. He was letting all our cousins into Heaven.

When it was my turn, he told me the next time a car drove by to pull my pants down. A car drove by, I pulled my pants down, and he sent me to Hell anyway.

In later years, if we were playing Monopoly and I somehow acquired Park Place and Boardwalk, Hugh would put hotels on his Railroads illegally and charge astronomical rents. When I squealed, he said, "Don't be such a brat," and I gave in. I somehow knew he had to win.

Like our mother, Hugh had a royalty complex. From the time he was born, he was captivated by kings and princes and popes, and he loved despots and palace intrigues and panoply. When he was fourteen, he retired from the family to an attic room at the top of the house, only leaving it for school and meals. He was a brilliant student, top of his class in English and physics, and he was endlessly creative with things mechanical and structural. His room, which I was once allowed to enter, was filled with gadgets, buzzers, bells, and a miniature theater with tiny spotlights and motorized curtains. He taught himself to play the piano; once in a while he descended from his lair, sat at the living room grand, and banged out "The Great Gate of Kiev" so loud the table lamps jumped. I didn't understand at the time that he was tortured because he was gay and his father treated him with contempt. He was filled with fury against both our parents.

As a grown-up he was both erudite and very funny, holding forth on such topics as Tristan and Isolde from the point of view of "poor King Mark," or on how Desdemona caused all the trouble because she lied about the handkerchief. At the same time, he could be physically hilarious, imitating a big-bottomed premiere danseur strutting around the stage or a mentally challenged king bopping his subjects on the head with his scepter. He considered being an actor for a while, but decided it wasn't a respectable occupation for a man. He became an English professor instead. Thank God. I could not have followed him onto the stage.

My sister Taffy had as little to do with me as possible while we were growing up. "Stay out of my room!" "Don't touch my things!" She was dainty, fastidious, with small feet and clean fingernails and all the boys fell in love with her—the exact opposite of me. Her funniness didn't seem to threaten her feminine charm. She could convey her opinion of something pompous or silly-looking with a grunt that made people burst out laughing. And she could move her body around like a soft custard, dancing to Zydeco, pallumping around the stage. She settled in New Orleans, raised three children, and was a much beloved actress in community theater productions. We stayed connected through the years, although she, like Hugh, couldn't ever quite bring herself to acknowledge my success. For years she sent me news clippings about actresses who had become drunks or thrown themselves out of windows.

Later, when the family came to see me perform, they were invariably at a loss for words. If I asked them how they liked the play or my performance, they looked uncomfortable and muttered something about the set or the music. When I once asked my sister about this, she said, "Well, maybe we're embarrassed."

It was inevitable that I should grow up believing the most important thing in the world was to make people laugh. It was the only thing. I had to get laughs. I got them in school by telling stories about myself. When people laughed I felt exonerated, relieved of my shame. At the same time, I was reinforced in my sense of lacking substance.

I often think of something I once read in a *Reader's Digest*: A colonel in India had a pet monkey that was pooping all over the house. The colonel proceeded to spank the monkey and throw him off the balcony every time he misbehaved, until finally the monkey learned after pooping to spank himself and throw himself off the balcony.

I constantly informed others of my flaws. It became a lifelong habit, a tic I wasn't even aware of. When anybody attempted to see something in me, I immediately felt it necessary to disabuse them. I had to keep my light under a bushel. On the other hand, when people took me at my word, I was furious. They were supposed to snuffle out my true worth without my help.

As an adolescent I was always getting lost, taking the streetcar the wrong way or taking detours to school, seeing men with their penises out and being terrified they would follow me.

I was ten when my mother embarked on the first of a succession of illnesses that would continue for the rest of her life. She developed an embolism in her leg and, on doctor's orders, she lay in bed in a darkened room for six months. Doctors also advised a couple of drinks a day "to keep her veins open." My siblings were old enough to escape after school to friends' houses. I came home to an otherwise empty house and my mother's moans and calls for more ice. I was in the sixth grade at Louise S. McGehee's School for Girls and I was out of control. I shouted in the halls, I couldn't stop talking, I was always in hot water because of something I said. One day I was called to Miss McGehee's office. Mummy was sitting there. She had gotten out of bed. She was wearing a fur piece I had never seen before. It seemed I had bullied a classmate so much that she had some kind of breakdown, and I was being expelled. Driving home, Mummy addressed the cosmos: "Any other mother would have thrown herself off a bridge."

*B*UT NOW HERE IS ONE OF THOSE MEMORIES THAT CONFLICTS WITH this view of myself as a totally despised miscreant. I must have been about twelve when I memorized the entire first act of *Arsenic and Old Lace*, playing all the roles—I practiced the lines in my bedroom closet so my siblings wouldn't hear—and I performed it, using a different voice for each character, at a parent-teacher meeting. It was a success, I repeated the performance at another adult gathering, and again it went over well. I don't recall the circumstances, who put me up to it, but it must have been an adult who noticed something good in me.

After this I was invited to enter a speech contest at a tiny college in northern Louisiana. My competition was a buxom girl who performed a dramatic poem called "The Highwayman." While reciting it, she impersonated the maiden with hands tied to the bedpost behind her so that with each cry of "The highwayman riding comes, riding comes!" she thrust her ample bosoms forcefully this way and that way, and she won first prize. This was my first taste of what I would be up against, so to speak, in future years. I came in second. My diploma read, "Second Prize (Comedy Division)." That last bit annoyed the hell out of me. It still does. Why is comedy not as respected as drama?

*A*ROUND THE AGE OF FIFTEEN I TURNED INTO SOMETHING OF A swan. I caught my family's sideways glances. They stopped laughing at my looks, at least. High school was more fun because of boys and dances. We were dancing to "Moonglow," "Mam'selle," and "Prisoner of Love."

Everybody read *Life* magazine in the forties. I loved the series "*Life* Goes To." The picture stories of New York City made a huge impression on me. One was a day in the life of a fashion model. The first photo showed a young woman gazing out her window while holding a cup to her lips. The caption read, "5:30 A.M. Betsy takes her last sip of coffee before heading out for her 6 A.M. modeling job." The next photo showed her standing on the curb with her hatbox in one hand—all the models carried hatboxes instead of purses—and waving with her other hand. "5:45 A.M. Betsy hails a cab" and so on through her day. There was "*Life* Goes to Broadway," which showed a young Julie Harris at an audition and a method acting class. I was also avidly listening to recordings of *Oklahoma!* and *South Pacific*.

Mr. Fredericks, the dour high school history teacher, had been assigned, I'm sure against his wishes, to put together a girl's cheerleading team. With some reluctance, he let me join. "You have great energy," he said, "you just need to *channel* it!" I didn't realize how much my insides jarred with my outside. I had a large presence, which was often scary to the gentler sort. Voice, gesture, everything about me was big. We were holding a pep rally for the football team in the auditorium because it was raining. In my new capacity as cheerleader, I got up on the stage and yelled, "Leeeet's go!!!" To my astonishment, the entire auditorium responded with a tremendous roar. Usually when I yelled, people yelled back "Shut up!" "Pipe down!" Now, for the first time, I experienced a positive power I didn't know I had.

One day in senior year, Mr. Fredericks stopped me in the hall and asked where I was going to college. I had no plans, my grades were atrocious. I probably would have followed the plan my parents had for me. Along with the other "nice" New Orleans girls, I would have gone to Newcomb College for two years, then made my debut, then probably married some drunk with an old family name, and ended up divorced or dead, if Mr. Fredericks hadn't said, "You should go to a college with a good theater school. You have talent." Nobody, no adult, had ever said such a thing to me. I applied to Northwestern University's School of Speech, and to my complete surprise, I was accepted.

NORTHWESTERN STUDENTS STRUCK ME AS CORNY. HORRIBLY RICH, Midwestern hayseeds. Cashmere sweater sets, Buick convertibles, mandatory sorority serenades, and Frankie Laine's "Mule Train" and "Cry of the Wild Goose" gave me the pip. Everybody drank Moscow Mules.

Question: Is mimicry the same as acting? Is the ability to become another person, to imitate, less than the ability to create a character from a written script?

By the end of freshman year, competition had knocked all the wind out of me. In New Orleans I had been the unchallenged clown among my classmates. Here, in the acting class you had to push and shove your way past everyone else to get your name up on the board in order to do a scene. And the scenes were from Odets and Lorca and Ibsen. I only wanted to be funny. I wanted to be Ado Annie. I came home on vacation and went to see Mr. Fredericks. I told him I felt like I wasn't an actress.

He shrugged and said, "Well, maybe you're just a mimic." I was crushed, to say the least. "Just a mimic" haunted me for years afterwards. I lacked the depth to be an actor. I couldn't cry on cue.

W HEN THINGS WEREN'T WORKING OUT FOR ME IN THE THEATER department, I switched my focus to English literature. Northwestern had wonderful English professors. I had never read a good book. In high school I passed up *Silas Marner* on the reading list for my mother's copy of *The Lovers of Lady Bottomley,* among other bodice-rippers she got from the library. I pored over *This Is My Beloved,* a steamy missive she had hidden in her underwear drawer. Now, I was devouring *Madame Bovary, The Magic Mountain, Crime and Punishment,* and *Ulysses.* The exams were generally "discussions": "Discuss Hans Castorp's declaration of love to Clavdia Chauchat"; "Discuss Emma's need for luxury"; "Why did she take a lover?" My God, "discuss!" I was the queen of bullshitters. I was getting As with red exclamation points on my papers. I discovered I had a brain. I decided to be an intellectual. I quit the sorority, played Brahms and Beethoven symphonies at top volume in my dorm room, and my roommate and I wore trousers and hung out in bookstores with guys who played chess.

This was when my brother Hugh began to accept me into his world. We were very much alike in looks and wit and rage against our parents. He saw me as his acolyte, I saw him as my lifesaver.

1950s: New York City

A FTER GRADUATION I CAME STRAIGHT TO NEW YORK AND MOVED into an apartment on West 114th Street with Hugh and his girlfriend Phyllis Starr. The apartment was dubbed "Fuchsia Moon Flat" because one of the Princeton aesthetes Hugh hung out with had said, "People like us meet only once in a fuchsia moon."

Philip, Wayne, Joel—these were his literate, witty young friends. I was thrilled to be included in their circle. They were my introduction to camp. There was much imitating of homosexual behavior, much wrist-flapping and lisping, "Get you, Ella." I thought it was so funny. I went around flapping my own wrist and lisping, "Get you, Ella." It didn't strike me as odd, much less offensive. I certainly didn't think that any one of them might be homosexual. I mean, here was Hugh's girlfriend, and then Philip kept flirting with me. Philip had a plummy voice and a mellifluous laugh; he kept grabbing me and tossing me around, gurgling, "I'll tame you yet, you gypsy wench!" Of course they were gay, but this was the fifties. You might as well have had smallpox.

We bought the furniture for Fuchsia Moon at the Salvation Army store on 125th Street, a veritable gold mine of mahogany dinner tables, bureaus, elaborately carved throne chairs, Tiffany lamps, and fumigated mattresses, as well as twenties evening gowns, fur coats, beaded dresses, Bakelite bracelets, feather boas, and fedoras that were bought for a song and put into the "drag chest" in our living room. Hugh, naturally, formed a court. He made crowns out of wire and beaten tin and we were given titles. Philip was the Duchess of Larchmont, Wayne the Duchess Biddy de Ripon, and Joel, Princess of Palestine. Phyllis was Princess of Panola because she grew up on Panola Street, and I was the Marchioness of Mauweehoo, which was the name of the lake in Connecticut.

Every morning the three of us put on our little seersucker outfits and trotted out the door to work. Every night we came home, climbed into the "drag," drank beer, and danced around the living room to Berlioz or Prokofiev or some other bombastic classical piece. There generally were a few straight friends—college acquaintances—hanging out on the sofa enjoying the show. Hugh sashaying around in a strapless evening gown with chest hairs sprouting from the top was a sight to behold. He was too hilarious to be seriously fruity. He was never serious about anything. It was forbidden. He talked about something he called the "emotionless criteria." I didn't completely get it, but the message sank in: no talk about your inner life or the state of the world, and no discussion of feelings.

I was terrified of the city. I had to get a job, but I couldn't imagine who would hire me, much less actually pay me. I was afraid I might starve to death. My roommates, both English majors, had editorial jobs in publishing. I figured the only thing I could be was a secretary but you had to know shorthand to take dictation. I tried pretending to do it on a couple of job interviews with humiliating results so I got my parents to cash in a WWII war bond they had taken out for me and I enrolled in a summer secretarial school on the fifteenth floor of the Radio City Music Hall building. In the classroom I became the same disruptive element I had been in high school, giggling over the corny inspirational sayings posted on the blackboard and being generally obnoxious. We were in a room high above the city taking dictation from the elderly instructor who would mutter "Dear sir," "Dear sir," and immediately drift off to sleep. We sat there, vacant summer sky floating outside the open windows and the voice of Mario Lanza singing "Be My Love" wafting up from the Music Hall far below until I couldn't contain myself any longer and burst out laughing and he woke up glaring at me. Needless to say I didn't graduate.

> *Thousands of women cut their hair because of her, cream their skins, shorten their skirts, and belt their coats—all at the iron whim of a woman whose face is as rarely photographed and as widely unknown as the other side of the moon.*
> Time *magazine, 1954*

I finally got my first job answering phones in a fashion photography studio, and, oh, those gorgeous models—Suzy Parker, Nina DeVoe, Jean Patchett, Dovima! They were trooping in and out of the office all day. I loved the charged atmosphere in that studio, the snits, the glamour of it all.

There were passing references to this powerful editor, I didn't catch the name, but I was an extremely style-conscious young woman and it was because of her that my hemlines went up or down by a fraction of an inch from year to year, to just below the knee, to the knee, or at the knee. One millimeter off from this year's hem spelled disaster: you were a total frump. The little sheaths I wore, the low-heeled pumps, short white gloves, a ribbon in the hair, these were hers, all hers. She told me when I could go without stockings in the spring, and how to tie a little scarf over my hair and behind my ears in the summer heat; she introduced me to thong sandals and, later on, the bikini.

At the same time this nameless source was being quoted in the confines of Fuchsia Moon:

> *Why don't you turn your old ermine coat into a bathrobe?*
>
> *Why don't you rinse your blond child's hair in dead champagne?*
>
> *Why don't you knit yourself a little skullcap?*

Hugh and Philip often quoted these infamous suggestions from the "Why Don't You?" column in *Harper's Bazaar*. Some people were horrified by the blatant trumpeting of excess. Humorist S.J. Perelman even published a lampoon of them. Our set understood Vreeland's intentional hyperbole. I still wasn't aware of who she was, though

> *I'm a great believer in vulgarity. We all need a splash of bad taste. NO taste is what I'm against!* —D.V.

IT WASN'T UNTIL A DOUBLE-PAGE SPREAD OF HER NEWLY DESIGNED living room appeared in *Harper's Bazaar* that I registered her name. Diana Vreeland's "Garden in Hell." I went nuts. This living room knocked everybody's socks off. You have to understand that in the fifties, the ruling décor of the day was beige; everything was beige or gray or modulations of beige and gray. The cardinal sin was to "clash." Now here was a veritable jungle of clash, crash, smash, brilliant red: red lacquered chairs; red floral chintz crawling up the walls and over the sofa and around the mirror, mixed with paisley, needlepoint, plaid, checks, and bargello; candelabra, pink tulips, paintings, blackamoor heads, gilt putti, horn snuff boxes, giant conch shells, and silver framed family photos littering every tabletop. Floral mixed with stripes! Leopard skin with crochet! You simply couldn't do that. It wasn't allowed.

When I thought about it later, I realized it was actually French decor. You only had to look at a room by Vuillard to recognize the patterns on top of patterns. But we didn't have jet planes back then. Nothing like it had been seen this side of the Atlantic before. For decades afterwards, this décor was so widely imitated by gay blades about town that it became a cliché.

I became more vividly aware of Vreeland in the early sixties, when she left *Harper's* to become editor-in-chief of *Vogue*. Hugh's girlfriend, Phyllis, was a copyeditor at Condé Nast at the time and came home with stories about her, swooping into the copy room on her first day purring, "*I want you all to write with quill pens!*" Another time she had a layout for little zippered satin jackets she planned to headline "The Windbreaker" until she was told at the last minute the word was patented. This time she roared into the copy room shouting, "*Quick! What's another word for breaking wind?*"

I'm always looking for the suggestion of something I've never seen. —D.V.

*I*DON'T RECALL WHEN MARK AND I DECIDED ON THE TITLE FOR OUR Vreeland play. I know it was pretty early on, and even when pressure was put on us to call it *D.V.* or *Think Pink*, or something equally as boring, we stuck with *Full Gallop*.

We started meeting on a regular basis, usually at my apartment. I always enjoyed being with Mark. He has a gift for empathy: any maddening or embarrassing incident I describe, he seems to instantly recognize and identify with. He has a biting sense of humor and a taste for the bizarre, for exaggeration. We kept our paying jobs, but for both of us, Mrs. Vreeland became our main thing.

The last thing we wanted to write was a bio-play. We didn't want to box this fantastic creature in with fact recitals. And it wasn't our goal to try to please her family. I didn't think we could do that. We even thought they might object to our version. My first idea was to write a sort of variety show with two handsome guys in tuxes on either side of her as she spouted her deathless pronouncements. This idea bit the dust almost as soon as it was out of my mouth. I remembered that one of the most annoying things about a one-person show is when he or she floats around in space. We decided, no matter how larger-than-life we wanted this to be, we had to anchor her somewhere, and the obvious choice was her wild and woolly living room, her Garden in Hell.

Not that this was going to be a one-woman show. There was no way we were going to do that. We despised one-person shows; in fact we originally got together to write a take-off of one, mocking the absurdity of the lone character having to supply their own exposition, talk to the air, make excessive use of the phone, and pretend that people were hovering just off-stage. There was the cautionary tale, perhaps apocryphal, of Tallulah Bankhead on tour in her one-woman show, stepping off left onto her balcony to talk to an unseen friend, and a voice from the audience calling out, "Invite him in!"

Besides, it's a well-known fact that one-woman shows, like comedy, and cats, get no respect. When it comes to awards, they're put in a separate category from plays. The Tony Awards don't even have a category for them. To avoid this stigma, we wrote a part for a maid, Yvonne. Mrs. Vreeland actually had an Yvonne, i.e., Françoise, for many years. The part was small but telling, she came in with drinks, shut and opened windows, brought in flowers, and emitted an occasional *"Oui, Madame."*

Beyond that, we believed that all we really had to do was select some of her stories and have her sit on a sofa and tell them.

Mark was prodigious. He put every single story in the book on a separate index card. We went over and over them, trying to decide which ones to use; we absolutely had to have her tell the one about entering the El Morocco on the arm of Clark Gable and his saying to her, "Hold on to your hat, kid, this place is gonna blow," and "as he said it, the place went berserk! . . . it was almost *animalique*. . . ." And I insisted on the one about announcing to her staff that she was going to devote a whole issue of *Vogue* to showing how to eliminate handbags, how women could keep their powder and lipstick and cigarettes in pockets "like a man does!" only to be reminded that two thirds of the magazine's income came from handbag ads. But in the end the story didn't fit. It was a heartbreaking process, because there were so many great ones that we couldn't use. We suffered from a surfeit.

SOMEBODY CASUALLY MENTIONED THESE METROPOLITAN MUSEUM videotapes to me, of two costume shows that Mrs. Vreeland had curated: "The Eighteenth-Century Woman" and "La Belle Epoque." I immediately went to the Met and bought them. I knew what she looked like, but I wasn't prepared for the impact of seeing her on these tapes. She was what the French called *jolie laide*, translated literally, "ugly pretty." Now in her seventies, she resembled a magnificently coifed camel. Her slicked-back black hair, her big rouged ears, her broad, expressive mouth, and her long, red-nailed, gesticulating hands were mesmerizing. Her strange Mid-Atlantic cum Brooklyn accent, her gravelly voice and her delivery, not to mention what she was saying, induced in me a mixture of awe and hilarity. This was a revelation of her personality. She was so much more than her pronouncements. Whenever the camera cut away from her I went crazy. Couldn't they see what they were looking at?

George Plimpton gave us copies of the audio tapes of his conversations with Mrs. Vreeland that he used for *D.V.* This was a veritable cornucopia. There were about twenty tapes, hours and hours of her talking, including asides to the maid, "Take this mess away," and genteel belches. I spent all of one winter listening to these tapes while painting my kitchen. For five years I walked along the country road by my house practicing her voice and speech patterns, telling her stories to the trees.

Mrs. Vreeland's friends spanned three decades; names that may be lost to time now but were once great: the Duke and Duchess of Windsor, Cole Porter, Elsa Maxwell, Coco Channel, Helena Rubenstein, Richard Avedon, Mick Jagger, Lauren Bacall, Jack Nicholson, Andy Warhol, Clark Gable, Jackie Kennedy, and she told wonderful stories about them. This was the beauty part; these were her spoken words with her own idiosyncratic syntax. She made up her own slang; Cecil Beaton remarked, "One would think she spent hours in ambiguous Times Square drug stores."

1950s: Nightclubs

I LOVED GOING TO NIGHTCLUBS IN THE FIFTIES. THE GLAMOUR! New York in the fifties and sixties had a great club scene. I saw Dorothy Loudon at the Blue Angel and Kaye Ballard at the Bon Soir, both gorgeous singers as well as superb clowns. I yearned to be up there myself, my face framed in the spotlight, the dark room full of piano music, cigarette smoke, and "women at their tables loosening their sables," as Bea Lillie once sang.

I saw a new act at the Blue Angel, Nichols and May. Elaine May's quavering voice and Mike Nichols's nasal whine were funny enough on their own, and their sketches were brilliant satires. There was something else utterly unique about them: they seemed to be making the lines up as they went along. This was New York's first exposure to improvisation, which was a new thing coming from Chicago with a comedy group called the Second City. This was also the first time I saw people performing skits in a nightclub with no singing, which was encouraging because I didn't want to have to sing in order to be funny. It seemed at that time that you couldn't do one without the other.

Most intriguing of all were these Julius Monk revues I kept hearing about. I fixated on them. I mooned over their write-ups in *The New Yorker*. They sounded like the ultimate in wit and sophistication. I finally found a date who could afford to take me to see one. The Upstairs room was shaped like a shoebox with red velour walls and a tiny stage at one end. The show consisted of clever musical numbers and funny sketches about New York life. The guys wore dinner jackets and ties and the girls wore black cocktail dresses and white gloves. So *insouciant*! So *soigné*! And all the time they were smiling out at me as if they knew me. Everyone, even the two pianists seated upstage at their spinets, seemed to be having the time of their lives—it gave me the notion there was a party going on just offstage, and any minute I might be invited in. The whole show passed by so swiftly and seamlessly, it was like a perfect soufflé. I thought it was the wittiest, most stylish thing going.

1991: First Reading of *Full Gallop*

NEAR MY HOUSE IN UPSTATE NEW YORK, SOME PLAYWRIGHTS, screenwriters, and actors I knew were forming a group to perform readings of their work. Their chosen name was straightforward enough: "Actors and Writers." Mark and I signed on for our first reading of *Full Gallop*.

At this point it was pretty simple: me as Mrs. Vreeland on a couch telling stories and giving orders to the maid. Mark wrote a fantastic prologue:

Magnified sound of water gurgling down a tub drain. (We played a magnified tape recording of water going down my tub drain. It was a wonderful sound effect.)

Sounds both muffled and magnified: murmurs, squeaks, fabrics rustling, snaps, bottle stoppers, etc. As lights come up behind a scrim, we see a maid at an ironing board ironing the contents of an Hermès handbag: Kleenex, dollar bills, etc.

Clouds of steam; out of the steam a figure emerges swaddled in towels.

A three-paneled screen appears. Maid and figure meet behind it. As the maid helps the figure dress, their actions are seen in silhouette. Bending down, stepping in, slipping on, zipping up. Their actions are expansive and ceremonial like Kabuki dancers.

Out from the screen steps an elegant figure, her head still wrapped in a towel.

A dressing table and bench appear. On the table is an assortment of cosmetic paraphernalia, and a mirror on a stand. The woman sits at the table. The maid stands behind her, hooks a huge makeup collar around the woman's neck, and executes a series of maneuvers on her hair as the woman applies makeup—a ritual involving jars, sponges, flacons, brushes, and culminating in a blizzard of powder.

She picks up her lipstick and leans into the mirror, a quadruple-magnifying glass which reveals to the audience the sight of a large red mouth.

The mouth speaks: "GREAT!" A red door appears in the scrim. The woman walks through it and Vreeland arrives onstage.

We had a battle over whether the audience would be able to read that the maid was ironing dollar bills; Mark insisted they could, and kept demonstrating, holding them up and waving them around. I didn't think her red mouth in the magnifying mirror would read either. Ultimately it was a nonissue, since at no point in our attempts to get the play produced was this prologue taken seriously.

Mark had set up an industrial sized fan in back of the audience, and during the reading he squirted an atomizer of Chanel No. 5 into the breeze over their heads. This was another one-time experiment; we were later informed that some people were allergic to scent. Despite or because of all this, the reading went over really well. People laughed! They loved this stuff! We hugged each other in glee. We sat down and started working on who we could send the script to, to get us produced.

Back in the sixties, in a summer stock production of *The Boy Friend* in Princeton, playing Alphonse opposite my Dulcie was Tyler Gatchell, a sweet, very funny thirteen-year-old with a terrible summer cold. Tyler was now a Broadway producer, but still just as lovable. I called him and asked if he would read our script. He said send it. We did. We heard back pretty quickly: we didn't have a play, we had a monologue. He added, "Ditch the maid."

We now realized we needed some kind of plot.

Tyler did give us a wonderful quote to use: Referring to her lipstick, she once asked a friend, *"Is it too much? Or not enough?"*

The Village

FUCHSIA MOON DISBANDED AFTER TWO YEARS WHEN HUGH, FEELING "hag-ridden," couldn't get far enough away from us. He moved to Wisconsin to get a master's in English literature. I was lost without him.

By this time, Philip of the "gypsy wench" business had made his way into the Greenwich Village theater scene and was beginning his career as a director. Philip Minor never had any money himself, was not well-known, but he was charming and cultivated, and he had a knack for befriending important people. I was once invited to his fourth-floor walk-up apartment on the unfashionable Lower East Side for dinner with Jason Robards Jr. and his then-wife, Lauren Bacall. It was like trying to converse with Jove and Hera. I could not bring myself to address her as Betty. I said something that she took great exception to, some stupid remark about Hollywood actors onstage. I thought she was going to leap from her chair and strike me. To this day I am extremely uncomfortable in the company of famous people. I invariably behave like an idiot.

I later learned that Bacall was discovered by Mrs. Vreeland. She modeled for her before going to Hollywood.

Once when I was clowning around, Philip said, "Mary Louise, you really ought to be in the theater." That was all I needed. Permission. He told me to come down to the Village and see this play *Summer and Smoke* at the Circle in the Square Theatre. This was the original Circle, on West 4th Street, opposite Sheridan Square. I loved the smell in there of rotting wood and musty velour. They passed a hat around for admission. I hadn't been in a theater like this before; the stage was a wide rectangle with plain wooden bleachers running along three sides; no set, no proscenium or curtain. We seemed to be in the same room with the actors. The main character, Alma, was played by an unknown actress, and as I sat watching her I felt I was eavesdropping. It gave me goose-bumps. It was partly the proximity, but it was also this actress, Geraldine Page. She was so real, so anxious and trembling and—palpable! I could have, I very much wanted to, reach out and touch her.

Then I took myself to see *The Threepenny Opera*, starring the great Lotte Lenya at the Theatre de Lys—now called the Lucille Lortel Theatre

—on Christopher Street. I had been reading Stephen Spender and Christopher Isherwood stories in college and this production—the rackety sound of the little orchestra, the grungy actors—was wonderfully authentic. The clincher was when Lenya sang "The Black Freighter," and lifted her arms high, revealing underarm hair. No woman in America in the fifties went around with underarm hair. To me, this was proof, if any more was needed, that she was the living embodiment of Weimar Germany.

I fell in love with the Village, the funky bars, the scruffy poets and actors. It brought out the beatnik in me. I moved into an apartment in a tenement on Barrow Street, around the corner from the Circle, for $90 a month. I had two roommates. One worked for Murray's Earth Shoes making plaster casts of feet which she brought home: tiny, twisted feet; beautiful feet; huge feet with hairs sprouting from the toes which we used for doorstops and bookends. We had orange burlap curtains and our chairs and tables were found in the street.

George Segal and his girlfriend, Marion, lived on the floor below us. The first time I saw George I was in awe of his leonine handsomeness, but he was completely disarming, funny and gregarious. He loved to play the banjo. "Yamma Yamma Man" was his big number. The Korean War was on, he got drafted and wangled himself into a "special services" unit. He put together a Dixieland band called Bruno Lynch and His Imperial Five. I still had my office job, but he made me the band singer, billed as "Pearl Fletcher, the Last of the Red Hots." We only played a couple of times, including a USO gig on Staten Island. The women's room was full of Spanish-speaking girls in bloated crinoline skirts yelling *"Mira! Mira!"* I stood up to sing "It's A Long Way to Tipperary," and I got as far as "It's a long way—" when a deafening roar went up. I don't know to this day if it was a roar of approval or the other, but I went sky-high on the lyrics and had to sit down. The ladies of the evening started yelling, "Marengue! Play marengue!" George had to put away his banjo and get out the maracas.

In what seemed like a week, George Segal went from serving lemonade in the Circle lobby to being a Hollywood star.

I went to parties with the Circle crowd and met José Quintero, Circle's brilliant director, a lean, charismatic Panamanian. I was accepted as Philip's friend, but I felt like a visiting debutante. There was no way I was going to give up my paycheck, but I prowled around the theater scene like a hungry animal.

I slipped into the Circle night after night to watch *The Iceman Cometh*. Jason Robards Jr. played Hickey. Hickey seemed so charming, such a great guy that I absolutely bought his message: "What have ya done to the booze, Hickey?" I thought it was the playwright's message, until Hickey imploded. During his epic monologue near the end, agonizingly, slowly revealing his crime, a drunk would cry out, "Aw, Hickey, get on with it!" and a mournful voice from the audience would occasionally echo, "Yeah, Hickey. Get on with it!" O'Neill was very long-winded.

But this was a thrilling production and Robards was superb. On opening night, I stood with a small group in the shabby lobby waiting for the *New York Times* review. When it came, Ted Mann, Circle's producer, read it aloud. It was a paean to O'Neill and to Robards. Jason had slipped out to get a beer, and just as Ted finished reading, he appeared at the top of the steps. We started cheering, yelling, jumping up and down. Jason stood there gaping at us, his hand moving to his chest, as if to say, "Me?" I knew I was witnessing a great moment. It was the making of the Circle, Quintero, and Robards.

My Last Office Job

AT THIS TIME I WAS A RECEPTIONIST IN ARCHITECT MARCEL BREUER'S office. Breuer was a kind, quiet man who called me "Mary Louis" and found me amusing. I loved being around these young, good-looking architects. I dated most of the single ones at one point or another. I was posing as a secretary; I managed to mess up the filing system so thoroughly that after I had been let go they had to call me back to straighten it out. And almost every day for three years, I arrived late for work. You have no idea how degraded I felt. It was simply not in my power to get up on time. I would sleep through the alarm, wake with a shout, dress in an awful panic, scrambling in the closet for a lost shoe or through a drawer for two quarters, ride the subway in a stupor, then try to slink to my desk unseen, only to meet the disgusted glare of my immediate superior. I felt like a bum. I'm sure they only kept me on as long as they did because I had good legs and I was fun at office parties.

1957: My First Theater Job

ONE DAY MR. BREUER SAID, "MARY LOUIS, I HAVE TO LET THE unmarried ones go." Almost that same day, Quintero called and asked me if I wanted to be in Circle's next production of *Our Town*. The pay was $27 a week. I played Second Dead Lady and Lady in the Audience Who Asks the Stage Manager If There Is Any Culture in Grovers Corners. My first professional stage job. I went up like a balloon. No more worries about oversleeping! No more riding the subway in rush hour! I could sleep late and hang out all day in leotards and sneakers in coffee houses! Oh, yeah.

THERE WAS SOMETHING PERFECT ABOUT A PANAMANIAN DIRECTing uniquely American plays by Eugene O'Neill and Thornton Wilder. In rehearsals for *Our Town*, Quintero rhapsodized to the cast in his Panamanian accent about the town, the morning, the evening, his arms extended, his beautiful, long-fingered hands suspended in flight, he wove a spell that embraced us all, from the leads to the paperboy with only one line. The play was another hit for Circle. Wilder himself came to see it, and when the cast came out to meet him, he ran toward us with his arms extended as if to embrace us all in one hug.

The Village Club Scene

*T*HE VILLAGE CLUB SCENE WAS THRIVING, EVERYBODY HAD AN ACT. Joan Rivers was trying out her material at the seedy Upstairs at the Duplex on MacDougal Street, and over at the Bon Soir this child Barbra came onstage wearing what looked like her grandmother's tea gown, opened her mouth and sang like an old black blues singer. We knew we were seeing something.

Another night at the Bon Soir a nerdy-looking guy, Woody something, got up onstage and did a very funny routine about his kitchen appliances, and once, late, I went into the Village Vanguard for a drink at the bar. It was between jazz sets, the place was almost empty, when this guy with a mike wandered onto the floor, stepping through a jungle of music stands and started holding forth. I thought, This guy is brilliant. Then I realized, "this guy" is Lenny Bruce.

Two actors, MacIntyre Dixon and Richard Libertini, had an act called "The Stewed Prunes" that was truly brilliant. Their sketches were like tiny Pinter moments:

> *Lights come up on a man slouched in a throne chair, head in hand. After an interminable silence comes a loud whisper from the wings: "Or NOT to be!" Lights out.*

The Threepenny Opera

WHEN *OUR TOWN* CLOSED, I HEARD THAT *THREEPENNY* WAS losing their Lucy Brown. Bea Arthur originally played Lucy. She sang the wonderful "Barbara Song":

> *Chin up high, keep your powder dry,*
> *Don't relax or go too far,*
> *Look, the moon is going to shine till dawn,*
> *Keep the little rowboat sailing on and on,*
> *You stay per-pen-dic-u-lar.*
> *Oh, you can't just let a man walk over you . . .*

The show had been running for two years; it was a rite of passage for many actors. In some cases it was a pit stop, in others a swinging door as, with much fanfare and many toodle-oos, someone would leave for a Broadway show that then flopped and back they came again.

Everybody was telling me I should go for the Lucy role. One afternoon I walked over to the de Lys and asked the stage manager if I could audition. He told me to come back with my accompanist and sing a song. I didn't have an accompanist. I hadn't ever had an audition, much less a singing audition.

Slightly prior to this, I had spotted this snappy-looking guy with round-rimmed glasses and a bow tie playing the piano at a party on the Upper East Side. I'd sidled over to him and shyly mumbled how I'd love to be onstage. Without looking up, still plonking away at the keyboard, he shot back, "Chutzpah, honey, you gotta have chutzpah!" What the hell was "chutzpah?" I didn't know. But a few days later, damned if I didn't spot this same guy going into the basement apartment of my building on Barrow Street. I knocked on his door and said I had an audition and asked if he'd play for me. He snapped, "It's going to cost you," and let me in.

This was the beginning of a long relationship with the eccentric performer and songwriter John Wallowitch. John had the distinction of playing for Faith Dane when she went up for the role of the stripper Mazeppa in the original *Gypsy* in 1959. He told me she auditioned in pasties and a G-string and blew taps on a trumpet through her legs. All of which, of course, ended up in the actual production. Those watching the audition were reduced to tears, including Gypsy Rose Lee, whose mascara ran black rivers down her cheeks.

For my *Threepenny* audition I wore a red dress, let my hair down to my shoulders, and sang Marlene Dietrich's "Falling In Love Again" in basso profundo, the only vocal register available to me at that time. As I was singing, I could see the stage manager out front shaking his head "no, no, no." Then I heard chuckling coming from the balcony. It was the director Carmen Capalbo, who just happened to be there that day picking up his royalty check. He came down the aisle and said, "You're very funny. What's your name?" He not only hired me to play Lucy Brown, he coached me, fixed my hair, even plucked my eyebrows. He loved the idea of discovering new talent.

Standing behind the curtain surrounded by *Threepenny*'s rollicking, raucous overture, I was thrilled out of my skull. This was real theater! Most of the grizzled character guys had been in the show since it opened. This was my first taste of "long-run-itis." Hands pushed and prodded me into my exact position in the gallows scene, as if footprints were painted on the floor. They instructed me on how to get my laughs: "Take a pause then say the line." "Stand like this, and then turn." I didn't get that at all. I only got laughs when I paid no attention to what I was saying. And I kept losing laughs because I didn't know how to stop paying attention to them.

I still get laughs when I don't mean to. The first time in front of an audience, I often get them. The other actors eye me suspiciously. Then the next night the laughs won't be as big, and the night after that, smaller, until finally they won't be there at all. I didn't understand why.

What did I do differently from the night before? I didn't have any control over it. For a very long time this made me extremely tentative about doing anything to meddle with my performance. I told myself to just stand there and say the lines. I agonized over this. I had to get laughs. I needed them. It was the only arrow in my quiver.

George Furth

*T*HE BARROW STREET BUILDING WAS CONDEMNED AND I HAD TO vacate my apartment. Up popped George Furth, an actor I knew, telling me about the empty apartment next door to his, on West 4th Street. George had a spastic energy, as if he were being repeatedly shot from a cannon. He was constantly telling me what to do: "You should put your hair up, wear makeup, and say 'blast!' instead of 'fuck.'" "I was talking to Hal Prince today, and he said if you stopped putting yourself down you could be the next Elaine May."

It was often some celebrity I didn't know that he claimed to be schmoozing with about me! It annoyed the crap out of me. "Dick Cavett says you should get your agent to send you up for leading lady roles."

George had been hovering near me since college. He was a class behind me, this pesky fly who kept diving into my face and shouting things.

After I came to New York he showed up at Fuchsia Moon. He was getting a graduate degree across the street at Columbia and he would drop by after seeing some Broadway play, and while I was practicing my shorthand, he would proceed to act it out, all the parts. As Linda in *Death of a Salesman* he shouted, "Attention! Attention must be paid to this man!" The windows were open, and someone across the alley shouted, "Hey George! Pipe down!"

I ended up moving into the apartment next door to George, and for the next few years we might as well have been living together. These were fifth-floor "cold water flats": toilet in a closet, tub next to the front door. The rent was $37.50 a month.

I was usually unprepared for George's onslaughts. He'd knock while entering, babbling. I hated that he could see the muddle I was in. On the other hand, he seemed not to notice, he was so filled with his own pronouncements. He couldn't hear me. If I told him I was thinking of killing myself, he would tell me about his lunch with Helen Hayes. It was like bullets ricocheting off steel. But at the same time that he was deflecting me, he was constantly telling me what I should do with my life.

George wore a rug; in those days you couldn't be balding and get young leading-man parts. He gave his rug a weekly shampoo, and while it dried he wore a towel topped by a golf cap. I had my hair up in giant rollers under a pink hairnet and together we ate Sara Lee coffee cake and watched *Queen for a Day* and *The Burns and Allen Show* on his tiny television set. The one thing we shared in spades was a passion for great comedy. We went together to see Bea Lillie in *High Spirits* and Ruth Gordon in *The Matchmaker*, hugging each other with delight over these two incomparable performers.

Still, I deplored George's taste. Helen Gurley Brown's *Sex and the Single Girl* had just come out and I was entertaining a new boyfriend, serving him a roast-beef dinner while wearing a ribbon in my hair, when he barged in with a canned pear floating in a green plaid dish. "I thought you might want this," he barked, giving my boyfriend the once-over. The thing that annoyed me most was the plaid dish. He had his entire apartment wallpapered in a beige print of Civil War soldiers, suitable for a schoolboy's bedroom. Horrible.

During a period of unemployment, George had been summoned downtown to report for jury duty and was officially declared a pauper. He was so unnerved he sat down and started writing these one-act plays. He showed them to me, but I didn't think they were very good. Eventually he showed them to Stephen Sondheim and they became the book

43

for the musical *Company*. Five years later, it opened on Broadway and George won a Pulitzer.

Full Gallop

WORKING WITH MARK ON THE PLAY MADE ME HAPPY. MRS. Vreeland was nourishing. We began finding other sources of information besides *D.V.* We heard about an interview she had with Lally Weymouth in *Rolling Stone* in 1977. In those days you looked at back issues on microfiche in the library. It was very difficult to get a copy to take away with you. It was like getting hold of the Dead Sea Scrolls. When we finally did, we read parts of it aloud to each other. It was a revelation. Up to this point I think we both thought of her primarily as a woman who told hilarious stories. Now we saw there was more to her.

> *There are so few things I really care that much about. I love my children . . . I really think about them every minute . . . I love my friends . . . and outside of that, life is wonderful and just charge ahead.*
>
> *I see nothing wrong with pleasure. I mean it sincerely. Perhaps I find pleasure where other people don't—I mean I get pleasure out of my bath, mad enormous pleasure . . . We were put here for the joy of it, for the hell of it, and it's all here now, nothing's been taken away, it's a question of creating it.*
>
> *I'm very conscientious . . . I'm very moral when it comes to work. I mean I have no sense of getting away with anything . . . You've got to be totally thorough, thorough, thorough, and it never occurred to me to be anything but that.*
>
> *Oh, you gotta have style. It helps you get up in the morning. It helps you get down the stairs. It's a way of life. I'm not talking about clothes. Money is a big help. But . . . no*

money in the world can produce that. There's got to be a mind and a dream behind it . . . It's innate, you know what I mean?

This last one took me years to grasp. I quoted it long before I thought to apply it to my own life.

The public at large saw Vreeland as a silly old gorgon in a turban shouting, "Think pink!" We fought this image all along the way to getting our play on.

An agent we submitted the play to wrote us that while she had enjoyed reading it, she was afraid that the subject had "no redeeming social value." She suggested a better subject might be Rose Kennedy. 'Nuf said.

More *Full Gallop*

I WAS CURIOUS ABOUT WHAT POWERFUL PEOPLE DID WHEN THEY LOST their high place. I once read a small item in the *Times* just after Clinton was elected; the ousted James Baker apparently approached Clinton about possibly staying on as Secretary of State. I thought, What chutzpah. What desperation.

When she came back from Europe, what did Vreeland do?

Mark and I went to Montauk for a long weekend in April to do some concentrated work. We stayed at the Montauk Inn and walked along the beach talking about how the ousted powerful find work. Mark fantasized a dinner party where influential friends throw out ideas; "Diana, why not design a line of bed linens?" "Diana you should start your own magazine! Call it 'D.V.!'" They would discuss ways to get backing.

At this point, we were so determined to avoid the biographical evening that it didn't even occur to us to use the facts surrounding the job she eventually got at the Metropolitan Museum. Looking back, it seems benighted of us.

How could we show who she was? She was no Madame Curie.

This is something that bothers me in solo shows, the character having to supply her own biography: "I was the most powerful fashion editor of the last four decades." "I invented electricity," blah blah blah. We couldn't have the maid do it. I became obsessed with the opening lines of the play. I wanted Vreeland's first words to give all the information needed: who what where when and why. We were going to have to resort to that tired old conceit, the telephone. We had sworn we would not use the telephone. In order to deal with this problem, Mark devised a brilliant gimmick. He invented an article in the *New York Post* which Vreeland picks up and reads aloud:

> *Brother Can You Spare A Diadem? Diana Vreeland, the recently deposed head of* Vogue *magazine, returned from abroad today with cup in hand.*

She throws the paper down at this point, but picks it up twice more during the evening, supplying more information. Everyone assumed we got the piece from the archives, but Mark made it up.

Another thing I loathe about solo shows is when the person onstage, supposedly in the privacy of her own bedroom, turns front and starts talking. She's addressing the cosmos. (When anyone at my family dinner table said, "Pass the salt," my grandmother would query, "Are you addressing the cosmos?") At least Mrs. Vreeland was in her living room, but she couldn't very well tell her life story to the maid.

So whom is she talking to? I saw the brilliant comedienne Pat Carroll in her solo show *Gertrude Stein Gertrude Stein Gertrude Stein*, in 1980. When she talked to the audience, I imagined I was attending one of her famous salons. Maybe Hemingway brought me along. On the other hand, *Tru* on Broadway in 1989 drove me nuts. Bobby Morse was so good he was heartbreaking, but the script by Jay Presson Allen had him home alone, yet playing to a theater audience. At one point he even went over to the curtain and fondled it, as if to say, "This is only a play."

I worried over this problem for months; we were lucky in that these were stories she had actually related, they had the feel of being spoken. I ended up making the audience a worshipful, unimportant young person whom she could ignore or confide in, could be uninhibited in front of, as her mood dictated. If I believed that enough, maybe the audience would, too. Beyond that, it would have to be a magic act.

1959: Julius Monk

I WAS IN *THREEPENNY* FOR ABOUT A MONTH WHEN GEORGE BURST in announcing that Jane Connell, one of the performers in Julius Monk's revue, was leaving to play Mrs. Peachum in Carmen Capalbo's West Coast production, and that I had to go uptown immediately and audition for her part.

Jane Connell was a goddess to me. With her blonde thatch of hair and her warbling soprano, her imitation of a folk singer rendering "The Race of the Lexington Avenue Express" was a masterpiece. Of course I refused. I was scared. I couldn't imagine myself being part of this glamorous venue that I worshipped from afar. I protested that I had just gotten into *Threepenny*. George went crazy; he wouldn't let up, he kept hammering away at me. He'd admitted that he had lied about Helen Hayes, but he was still genuinely adept at befriending big names, and now he got famous people I didn't know, like Burr Tillstrom of *Kukla, Fran and Ollie*, to call me. (When I told this to John Wallowitch, who thought I should stay with *Threepenny*, John snarled, "Did Burr tell you about his whips and chains?") Anyway, I finally buckled.

The Upstairs at the Downstairs was on West 56th Street, just off Fifth Avenue. I was told to arrive at 10 P.M., between shows. The bar area just inside the door was jammed with people laughing, shouting over each other. A tall, distinguished-looking gentleman, beautifully dressed, came toward me through the crowd. This must be Julius, the man I came to sing for. He was speaking to me in an accent: British? Southern? Southern/British? Southern/British/Affected? His words came out in soft hoots from under his impeccable mustache. I couldn't make out what he was saying. He led me into the red-draped Downstairs room, empty except for a gracious young man seated at the spinet piano. I handed him my sheet music. I was scared witless. I stood on a tiny stage in front of the piano and launched into my comedy number, "Something Wonderful" from *The King and I*. The song was originally intended as a loving tribute to the King by one of his many wives, but I took it a bit further and sang it as an abused woman. On the words "he will not always do just what you'd have him do," I cringed and rubbed my arm. While singing "he has a thousand dreams that won't come true," I looked over my shoulder and hissed in terror. Was it going over? I think I saw his mustache twitching. In my crazed performance I shouted the high notes, and at the end I flung my arm out in a wild gesture and knocked a pitcher of water into the innards of the piano. Mr. Monk remained unflappable. He invited me to sit down at the table with him while a sweetly smiling waiter swabbed up the water. The waiters, everybody, seemed to be smiling sweetly.

I still couldn't understand a thing Mr. Monk was saying. Every now and then a word was hooted into the clear—"tessetura," "rodomontade," "post-prandial." I couldn't tell if he was hiring me or letting me down. Then he took me upstairs to meet the cast, and I thought, Well, he must be thinking about hiring me, if he's doing this. He knocked on the dressing room door, the Inner Sanctum. It slid open and there they were, my idols, smiling out at me. I couldn't believe I could be one of them. At the same time, I knew this was exactly where I belonged.

We rehearsed in the Upstairs room. I loved the smell in there of stale booze and cigarettes. The maitre d', poker-faced actor Bruce Kirby, stuck his head in and said, "You kids keep it quiet up here." When Bruce seated women customers who asked "What do I do with my fur?" he recommended they have the hem taken up or down a couple of inches.

Julius Monk had the title of each sketch and each musical number written on Tiffany notecards, which he propped up on a table in front of him: little white tents that he moved back and forth, playing chess with the running order. His secret talent was knowing how to follow an act. If, during previews, one of us had a number that elicited too much applause, he would move it to another position, which was mystifying to me at the time. He wouldn't use sketches that were too hilarious. No showstoppers allowed! His reasoning was that the show had to flow as one continuous unit. I remembered when I saw it being charmed by the way the whole thing moved seamlessly from beginning to end, no one performance standing out above another.

Julius's other cardinal rule was that we could not play to each other. We must never exclude the audience. It came to me that this was why, when sitting out front, I felt flattered by the performers. Because of the eye contact, people often greeted us on the street like old friends. Carol Channing waved to me in a restaurant, "Hi, Mary Louise, it's Carol." As if I didn't recognize the large blonde head, fake eyelashes, and big red mouth!

The first night I went on, I looked down at the front table and Noël Coward was smiling up at me. Famous faces dotted the audience every night: Tennessee Williams, Esther Williams, William Carlos Williams, Ava Gardner, Gregory Peck, Charlton Heston, David Frost, Robert Frost, Montgomery Clift, Arthur Miller, Ann Miller, Roger Miller, Ginger Rogers, Richard Rodgers. Once we spotted a pair of elegant mummies sitting in a corner banquette: the Duke and Duchess of Windsor. All the theater people, producers, casting agents, as well as actors were there.

Even couched in this fabulous situation I found myself casting longing glances at another newer show in town called *The Second City*. While our every word and gesture was choreographed, these great young players, among them Alan Arkin, Bob Dishy, Robert Klein, and Barbara Harris, apparently made their lines up as they went along. It was unheard of, a kind of controlled chaos, very funny and it looked like heaven to me. Actors are never satisfied: When they're acting in a tragedy they're longing to be in a comedy. If they're on the stage they want to be on TV, if they're on TV they want to be in film, if they're in film they want to be on stage

I did three seasons of these shows, two shows nightly, seven days a week, from September through May. Three years. The pay was minimal but we had our summers free, and we could collect unemployment and go to the beach knowing we had a job in the fall in the hottest show in town. Most of the waiters in the club were actors, and after the last show at night we went out drinking together. One of them—tall, blue-eyed Bob Downey Sr.—was my boyfriend for a while. Bob was gorgeous. He was the original hippie. His bible was *Catch-22*. He called me "Bitch"—riding past me on his bike he would yell, "Hey, Bitch!" Bob had maybe the first underground newspaper, mimeographed, in which he made outrageous claims: the powerful columnist Dorothy Kilgallen had a mustache; the Pope was gay. He made a movie starring himself as a Yankee soldier who wakes up in the present in Central Park. In one scene, he walked onto the field at Yankee Stadium in his uniform in the middle of a game and got arrested.

I marveled that I could stay out until five in the morning and show up to perform that night fresh as a baby. Of course, I *was* a baby. Julius was our daddy. The cast was my family; its members changed slightly from show to show, but a basic core remained. We even spent our days off together, as there was precious little free time for outside friends or lovers. At one point, and briefly, two of us went so far as to become lovers.

Lovelady Powell

*I*WAS A MISERABLE FRESHMAN STANDING ALONE SMOKING A CIGA-
rette in Northwestern's Theta house during sorority rush week
when a tall, hefty girl leaned her friendly face into mine and said,
"You're majoring in theater! So am I!" I was so unnerved by this unexpected attention I spit a piece of tobacco and to my horror it landed
on her cheek. She didn't flinch. She went right on talking, making me
feel less lonely. Her name was Lovelady Powell. In the big college
musical, the WAA-MU Show, she did a wonderful imitation of Carol
Channing singing "Diamonds are a Girl's Best Friend." She graduated a year before me. Soon after I arrived in New York, I was taken
to a nightclub called the Purple Onion on Sixth Avenue and 53rd St.,
the future site of the Time-Life building. There was a hot new
chanteuse singing there. She slithered into the spotlight, a sinuous,
glamorous wraith all in black with an Audrey Hepburn boycut, clown-
white face, kohl-rimmed eyes. Her mouth a red gash. She crooned
her songs in a kind of anguished method-acting style, occasionally
wrapping her limbs around a pole. I was transfixed. Suddenly in the
middle of a song she looked right at me and waved. At me? I looked
behind me. Yes, she was looking and waving at me. She was Lovelady
Powell. I was flabbergasted. She had transformed herself into this
slinky songstress. Lovey was getting noticed, she had a good thing
going when her arranger and accompanist was suddenly drafted. The
Korean War was on. Apparently her arrangements were all in her accompanist's head. Nothing written down. So that was that. I recall she
had a short period of making do. She lived for a while in the same
cheap tenement George Furth, Ruth Buzzi, and I were in. She went
down to Chinatown and bought a huge bag of rice to live on. Lovey
never did anything in a small way. She had great style, tremendous
energy and everything she did was big and beautiful. She wasn't broke
for long. She was in Julius Monk's shows, she played the female foil

to Danny Kaye on his television show. She raised wire-haired terriers, gave lavish cocktail parties, served caviar in vats the size of bathtubs. She changed apartments like hats, beautifully decorating them. Once she saw Bergdorf Goodman's windows full of palely colored old shutters, the kind once used for hiding construction sites, and she bought them all. I can't recall where she put them, maybe along the walls of her newest living space, a floor in an old warehouse on Coentes Slip before human habitation down there was even dreamed of. I think this was when she bought a motor scooter. We were both working at the Upstairs. After the show I hitched a ride downtown. It was heaven gliding down an empty Avenue at two a.m. in the balmy September dark, waving to Con Edison men as we passed.

1960s: Television Commercials

*J*UST WHEN I WAS THINKING HOW FABULOUS, HOW CUSHY IT WAS to lie around in *dishabille* all day and then rise to perform at night in the most glamorous venue in town, along came television commercials. Ad agencies were switching from using models to what they called "flawed faces," meaning us, the Cute and the Funny, in their commercials. It annoyed the pants off me that here I was, in the sweetest gig in town, and now all of a sudden I had to troop up to Madison Avenue to audition for these things. It seemed like every job was looked on as merely a springboard to the next one. It was considered *de rigueur* for actors starring on Broadway to go downtown after their shows to perform their club acts. This kind of thing exhausted me just hearing about it.

I reacted particularly badly to being routed at 9 A.M. with a phone call, "Can you be uptown in half an hour looking pretty?" I felt unfairly harassed. But the night Lovelady swept into the club with an artichoke haircut and a long pink feather boa because she had become the Listerine Lady, I put my pants back on and started showing up.

Everything I know about walking I learned from watching Ziegfeld's girls. —D.V.

Julius at the Plaza

IN 1962, JULIUS MOVED HIS REVUES FROM THE CLUB ON WEST 56TH Street to the former Rendezvous Room at the Plaza Hotel, and everything got the lavish treatment. The room was gutted, painted red, and renamed the Plaza 9 Room. We women were in evening dresses and the men wore tuxedos, the pianists sat at baby grands on either side of the stage, and like so many good things when they hit the big time, the show lost its edge. Our loyal fans who followed us from the Upstairs at the Downstairs were being served much bigger drinks on the two-drink menu, and coming backstage unintentionally plastered.

Still, I was excited by the glamour of it all, wearing designer gowns, being photographed for *Vogue* magazine, rehearsing in the hotel's white Moire Room with its white baby grand. Every afternoon the management would roll in a tea trolley loaded with crustless sandwiches, petit fours, tea, and champagne. But the sketches weren't as witty. We sang a chivvying anthem to the Plaza, to its chandeliers and candelabras, as if it were the Cradle of Civilization.

I was getting a lot of attention. What was expected of me? Being considered for television shows like *Laugh-In* and *The Garry Moore Show* scared the hell out of me. In one Julius Monk revue I had this ditty called "Names," with lyrics that went something like this:

> *If Conway Twitty would marry Kitty Carlisle,*
> *Then Kitty Carlisle would now be Kitty Twitty.*
> *If Faye Emerson had married Johnny Raye*
> *When the wedding was done, we'd have another Fay*
> *Wray . . .*

and so on, verse after verse, each with slight grammatical variations. These names, so dead now, were of course well-known back then.

I was doing fine with the song, then one night we heard Garry Moore was out front. The Garry Moore television show featured a young comedian, Carol Burnett, who was leaving to do her own show, and it was rumored that Mr. Moore was shopping for a replacement. I came out and started to sing "If Conway Twitty would marry Kitty Carlisle, then Kitty Carlisle would now be Kitty Twitty—" and stopped cold. There was nothing in my head. The twin pianos behind me clattered to a stop, I looked at the audience and said, "I can't remember." The audience let out a unanimous "*Awwwwww*," and someone yelled, "Start again!" I knew it was no good, the words had left the building. They were down the street. Out of town. Then a voice, Garry Moore's, called out, "Just sing, Mary Louise." So I started again and stopped again. I mumbled an apology and barged offstage. I was mortified. I stifled the thought that I had screwed up on purpose.

On opening night of the Plaza 9 show, Rowan and Martin, creators of the television show *Laugh-In*, came backstage during intermission and asked to meet me. I was terrified. I hid in the dressing room. Ruth Buzzi, who lived below George and me in the West 4th Street building, was now a regular on their show, and she scolded me for turning down this chance. I didn't understand why she was so mad. I knew it was a big deal, but the performers on *Laugh-In* all seemed to have their "bits," their little characters. I couldn't just "be funny," I needed a script. No script would be like having no net. At least Buzzi had her hairnet. So I argued to myself, but I felt guilty. I should want to be chosen.

Meanwhile, world events were getting too ugly for polite satire. I had a Scottish Highland number about "Bonnie Patrice Lamumba comin' lightly o'er the Lea" that had to be pulled because in Africa Patrice Lamumba was having his speeches stuffed in his mouth and set on fire. And backstage, my lover had left me for a new cast member and I was in agony watching them necking in the wings every night. When I got a part in a Broadway show, I was more than ready to leave.

In the sixties you were knocked in the eyeballs. Everything was new. You had the jet, you had the pill. —D.V.

1963: Hot Spot

THE PART WAS JUDY HOLLIDAY'S BEST FRIEND IN *HOT SPOT*. JUDY Holliday was a fabulous comedienne, and a huge star on Broadway and in film.

I saw myself as being on my way. At some point I would arrive. I didn't know what would happen then. I assumed I would be some place great and I would stay there. My success so far had seemed effortless. Without doing much of anything, people found me funny. I was afraid to mess with that. Besides, I didn't know what else to do. I saw it all as happening to me.

I signed with an agent, Richard Astor. I knew I wanted to sign with him when I saw on his wall a black and white photograph of Beatrice Lillie holding a calla lily to her ear and speaking into another calla lily. Richard was Lillie's American agent. When he called to say I got the part, I galloped around the room singing, "They want me! They want me!" That was a mistake. I have since learned that it is seldom, if ever, "they" that want you. During the entire run of the show, Miss Holliday spoke to me exactly once: just before her entrance on opening night in New Haven, she looked at me and hissed, "Salts!" I misunderstood and whispered back, "You too!" Later I realized that she must have been feeling faint. Apparently she had wanted another actress for my part.

From the outset, the show was divided into enemy camps. On one side was the lyricist Marty Charnin, the composer Mary Rodgers, and the book writers, Jack Weinstock and Willie Gilbert; on the other side was Miss Holliday and her friends. I knew which camp I was in. At the same time I felt bad for her. It was a lame excuse for a book. At the first rehearsal, Marty Charnin stood up and announced exultantly, "We have no second act!" and to my amazement everybody laughed and applauded. There never was a second act. The plot as such was about Peace Corps volunteers landing on a native island. By the end of this debacle, the chorus had come up with several brilliant second acts. The best one had the island natives making their living selling porn films. Originally the singers were the Peace Corps and the dancers were the island natives, but by the third week out of town and umpteen-billion rewrites, some dancers' gorgeous limbs were shrouded in baggy khaki and knee socks while some singers waddled around in grass skirts, their tubby bodies smeared in Texas dirt makeup. There was a gigantic curtain made of rope. Every time it hit the floor, rope particles flew into everybody's throats.

By coincidence, George Furth had also been cast in the show. At one point in all the script adjustments, for no discernible reason, they changed his character name, which sent him howling down the hotel hallway. There were so many script changes that the cast was making airplanes out of them and shooting them out of the hotel windows.

Hot Spot had more directors than you could shake a script at. Judy kept firing them. The original director was Morton "Teke" DaCosta, an affable gentleman noted for his un-interfering direction of diva vehicles. He disappeared after the first preview. When I asked the British stage manager what happened, he said, "He was bleeding from the *ahhss*, darling." And then began the parade, a veritable who's who of theater directors who came to our try-outs in New Haven, D.C., and Philadelphia to try to fix us. A director would take the train from New York to see the show, come backstage and give the cast a pep talk, the cast would applaud, then he would meet with Judy and not be seen again. When Arthur Laurents came he told us, "Listen, I just came from skiing in the Alps. When you're skiing you have to be careful or you can fall and break your ass. Well, we're not going to do that with this show!" Big applause. The next morning the cast arrived to rehearse, and there was a note on the sign-in board: "He fell and broke his ass.— The Management."

Meanwhile, Miss Holliday kept dumping her scenes. In the end she didn't even have one with her leading man. Her boyfriend at the time, saxophonist Gerry Mulligan, told her, "You're a singer, babe, you don't need scenes." When we got to New York, the film director Herbert Ross came onboard and stuck. Maybe he had guessed the Riddle of the Sphinx.

Every scene Miss Holliday dumped, the writers had given to me, and now, two days before the New York opening, they were all taken away. No explanation. I remember George yelling "That's not fair!" Not that there was ever a chance of me casting so much as a breath of a shadow on her.

The show now consisted entirely of a series of big musical numbers separated by "crossover scenes," with George and me down in front of the curtain, which lasted just long enough for Judy to change costumes and take a drag on her oxygen tank. New numbers were being ghostwritten by friends. Once, coming into rehearsals, I saw a man sitting onstage astride a chair wearing a homburg, dove grey gloves, and a jaunty smile. Adolph Green. I'd swear he was also wearing spats, but probably I just dreamt that.

On opening night in New York, in our dressing rooms getting ready, the cast was rattled to hear completely unfamiliar music. Were we in the right theater? Stephen Sondheim had written a new opening number that afternoon. Judy had been dragging through the show for weeks, but this night she rose like a phoenix and gave a tremendous performance. She got great reviews. The show closed three weeks later.

After *Hot Spot* closed, George signed a players' contract with 20th Century and moved to Los Angeles. I thought, Great! He always wanted to be in movies, and now at last he's off my back. No more bursting into my apartment unannounced and telling me what to do with my life. But I wasn't prepared for living next door to his empty apartment. For the first time since coming to the city, I was on my own. Nobody was around. Nobody was interested in telling me what to do.

Twice Over Nightly

*I*N THE FALL OF 1963, I WAS IN AN IMPROVISATIONAL REVUE WITH MacIntyre Dixon and Dick Libertini of the Stewed Prunes, Paul Dooley, and a three-months-pregnant Jane Alexander. We wanted to call it the William Howard Taft Memorial Revue, but the club owner balked and renamed it Twice Over Nightly, which sounded almost as anarchic. There were some really funny sketches in this show, but there was no publicity and nobody came to see us. Paul Dooley used to introduce the show, "Good evening, lady and gentleman," or sometimes, "Good evening, table and chair."

I was putting on my socks watching television on my little television set when the news broke in: President Kennedy had been shot. All of the following week it seemed the world did nothing but watch television, replays over and over again of the cavalcade at Dealey Plaza, the shooting of Oswald, and the funeral. Jackie Kennedy in a black veil bending over her little boy raising his arm in salute. It seemed as if everything changed after that. There was the world before and the world after. A lightness, a gaiety, was gone forever.

The maharajas were a dime a dozen. They put jewels on their elephants. On their elephants! Do you realize what an elephant is today? They're even hard to find in India! During the coronation in London we saw them go by like taxis on Park Avenue. —D.V.

Full Gallop

AFTER THIRTEEN YEARS AS EDITOR-IN-CHIEF OF *VOGUE* MAGAZINE, Mrs. Vreeland had been fired. We were curious about what she did immediately afterwards. We knew it had been a blow, a bomb dropped. There were conflicting accounts. George Dwight told us she took to her bed for six months. Someone else said she went to Europe for four months with her friend Kenneth Jay Lane, the high-society costume jeweler. Somehow we wangled an audience with this man.

We were ushered into the living room in his mansion on Park Avenue, an enormous octagonal seraglio swathed in drapes, sofas, pillows, and poufs, and there he was, semi-recumbent in a Savile Row suit, sucking on a cigarette. His speech was a startling replica of Vreeland's. While he talked, the ash on his cigarette dangled perilously over his impeccable shirtfront; I kept resisting the urge to leap forward and catch it, but he would pull the cigarette away just before it dropped.

Kenneth told us a story about Vreeland's search for a certain shade of blue. She could see it in her mind but she couldn't find it in the real world. Friends were calling her and saying, "Diana, is it the blue of the Aegean you're looking for?" She was driving everybody crazy trying to find this color blue. Friends suggested the blue in the Fragonard skies at the Frick, the blue of the little boiled snails in Corfu, the blue of the Duke of Windsor's eyes—she had once said there had never been a blue like the blue of the Duke of Windsor's eyes—but to all of these she shouted, "NO! No, that's not the blue I'm looking for!"

Finally, Kenneth called her one day and said "Diana, do you remember that time a few years ago when we were up in the hills above Antibes, we were riding on these charming little donkeys, and the donkeys had those beads around their necks, those blue beads?" There was a long silence on the other end of the line, and then a deep, conclusive, "Donkey."

He told us that the entire time they were in Europe, she said nothing about what had happened and was usually up for fun, except for one night in Madrid. She told him that he should go out to dine without her, that she was tired, would dine early in the hotel dining room, and then retire. He offered to keep her company while she ate. The dining room was almost empty, it was only eight o'clock, and the Spanish didn't dine before ten. They were sitting there when an orchestra in the lobby started to play. Through the doors they heard the faint strains of "Fascination," an old familiar tune. He glanced at her; tears were streaming down her face. He told us, "She didn't say a word, and neither did I."

I wondered if her tears were because of her job loss, or was it the memory of hearing this tune with her adored husband, Reed? Who knows? That's what I love about her. Some things remain a mystery. Was she really born in Paris? Did Lindbergh really fly over her lawn in Brewster, New York? Some people thought it was their duty to prove her a liar. Who cares what the truth was? She found fantasy much more interesting. She was born in Paris, but real facts bored her so that when interviewers asked, she made up birthplaces: Vladivostok, Kathmandu, Timbuktu. She was a reporter who saw herself as being there on the spot when big things were happening. She was there when the international playboy Alfonso de Portago was seen kissing the film star Linda Christian just before driving off in a car race and losing his life in a spectacular crack-up. She was there when Cole Porter's horse fell on him and broke his legs.

As for her tears, was she not, as some said, like so many fashionistas, incapable of deep feeling? Or was it that she didn't believe in showing her grief? Her beloved father used to say in bad times, "Worse things happen at sea." In any case, we determined that the time for our play to take place would be just after Vreeland had been fired.

Acting Lessons

I WAS AUDITIONING FOR THE LEAD PART IN MUSICAL AFTER MUSICAL and not getting hired. One thing that didn't help was the current call for "kookie." Goldie Hawn on *Laugh-In* was "kookie," meaning funny and cute. Not in anyone's wildest dreams could I pass for kookie. Much less cute. "Ethnic" was another big casting trend. I blame "ethnic" on Barbra Streisand, who was zooming past us on her way to the stratosphere. In her wake, it became the thing to have a New York accent. Somehow if you had a New York accent you were more believable. I was a hopelessly well-spoken Presbyterian.

I had no clue what I was doing. I had nothing to hang on to, I was going out there on a wing and prayer. I decided to take some acting classes. In the 1960s, there were three major acting schools: the Actors' Studio; HB Studio, run by Herbert Berghof and his wife, the renowned actress Uta Hagen; and the Neighborhood Playhouse, run by Sanford Meisner. I signed up to study with Uta. The first scene I did was from a J.D. Salinger story, which took place between an adolescent and her older sister's boyfriend. I remembered when I was that age, having a self-conscious fixation on my big feet in their orthopedic shoes. On instinct, I concentrated on my feet through the whole scene, and every line got a huge laugh. Uta roared. Following protocol, we repeated the scene the next week, but this time there was not a laugh in a carload. What happened? Uta would surely know, she would be able to tell me what was different, but she threw her hands up. She had no idea. Comedy was not her strong suit. She assigned parts to me to work on, like

Hilda Wangel in *The Master Builder*. Uta's method to make it real was to study the boots Hilda wore, maybe she had corns from all her walking to get to that house; and her corset, maybe it itched; her hair, what soap she used; her surroundings, family illnesses, the weather, all the minutiae, the physical facts. But Ibsen was miles away from me, across a vast expanse of ocean. I hated Ibsen.

A year or so later I started taking classes from Sanford Meisner. "Sandy." Sandy had this exercise he was crazy about, and had us doing it for weeks on end. It was called the "repeat" exercise. Two actors sat facing each other; one said something mundane like, "You have brown hair," and the other repeated the words back, then he repeated them again, and so they would go back and forth for an interminable length of time. The object obviously is to learn to respond to the tone of voice rather than the words. It can be very boring, but it helped me enormously.

Sandy, like Uta, gave us scenes from podgy old plays like *The Children's Hour* and *The Gordian Knot*, but when I was doing a scene in class I just concentrated on that one thing, what the other actor was giving me. Sandy's favorite saying was, "Acting is reacting." His other favorite was, "Acting is behaving truthfully in imaginary circumstances." He helped me join in my mind being funny with being truthful.

One day Sandy stood in front of us and told us about his vacation cabin in the Maine woods, how he got up at dawn and raced down to the frigid lake and jumped in, how he made a wood fire and cooked an enormous breakfast, flapjacks and syrup he got himself out of his maple trees, and on and on until we were mesmerized, and then he said he made it all up. He actually had a place in the Bahamas. He was not a proponent of sense memory, the idea of which had always made me squirm. The few times I observed it in various other classes I had dropped in on, people were reliving their rape scenes and such with abandon and I felt personally violated. He believed that emotions could be called up by the imagination. Everybody fantasizes, whether it's the thrill of getting a role in a play, or the pain of a pet or person dying.

One time a student was supposed to enter in a scene, but she was taking a very long time. Sandy called to her; she said she was supposed to enter screaming but was having trouble calling up the proper emotion. He said, "Go out, shut the door, and just come in screaming."

He reminded me of the forties' comedian Jack Benny. He stood in front of us, contained and dapper with his hands folded in front of him, and when a student rudely asked, "What do you do in a real play when the other actor won't work with you?" he turned his head to one side, rolled his blue eyes to the ceiling, and gave a huge shrug. Sandy had no interest in the current theater world. In fact he despised it. The only people he praised were the famous lieder singer Dietrich Fischer-Dieskau, and the actress Kim Stanley in *Séance on a Wet Afternoon.* I believed he liked me, and saw something in me. When I left class to go to Cincinnati to play Lady Would-be in Ben Jonson's *Volpone,* he did not approve. He was right—I probably would have learned more if I had stayed with him.

I never wanted to be in the center of the spotlight. Too much expectation. I saw my niche as Best Friend to the Star; the Sidekick. The Über Sidekick was film actress Eve Arden, sitting on the sofa arm, clutching a foot-long patent leather purse, and making wisecracks out of the corner of her mouth while Joan Crawford chewed the scenery. And on stage there was Alice Ghostley, Jane Connell, Nancy Walker, and Bea Arthur. They weren't the stars, they were "the best things in it." I liked that idea.

The problem is that the show business you dreamt of is never the one you end up in.

Queen Mary's hats looked as though they could be taken off and used as something—to dust the house.

—*D.V.*

1964: Sherman, Connecticut

SHERMAN, CONNECTICUT, WHERE WE SPENT OUR CHILDHOOD summers, was Eden. My father had built a cottage with plans from a Sears and Roebuck kit up the hill behind his parents' farmhouse, and we summered there on and off from the time I was born until the sixties. There were birthday parties and picnics and swimming and fireworks. The sight of watermelons cooling in the brook filled me with excitement: soon I'll get what I'm missing, soon I'll be happy! For years afterwards, it remained a time and place I longed to be.

Later in our twenties when we went there, my mother and brother would become locked in combat over house chores, mowing, raking, painting, etc. One night in the living room, all of us drunk, Mummy on the sofa sounding off for the fiftieth time about how she was going to "sell this house." Hugh grabbed me in the kitchen and snarled, "Remember King Lear!"

When he and I were living in New York we came up on weekends with assorted friends. Hugh was Captain of the Games. For birthdays and holiday celebrations, he blew up the balloons and chose the music and broke out the costume trunk. We put on all the hats and cloaks and Mardi Gras ball gowns and gaudy finger rings from Woolworth's. Sometimes we spent so much energy getting into costumes and crowns and rings and things that, once completed, there was nothing left to do but sit there. It was exhausting. Hugh made films with my father's 16mm camera starring Philip, Phyllis, me, and himself. "Frenzy in Old Rome" was one. It was set to the music of Prokofiev's "Symphonie Fantastique" and we caromed around the local cemetery in bedsheets. The film was about seven minutes long.

Hugh was attached to the house, I thought probably for the same reason I was: the promise of something he never got. In 1964, our parents sold it to us for a dollar and we took out a mortgage on it and gave them the money to retire to Santa Fe. The first thing Hugh did was throw all of Mummy's pots and pans out of the kitchen window. We were free at last from her constant demands to wash the dishes, mow the lawn, set the dinner table, empty the garbage, and paint the porch. I thought we'd just go on living there as carelessly as we always had. I wanted to hang on to the past, wanted the house to stay the same with its cramped little bedrooms upstairs under the rafters, it's mattress-ticking sofa, rickety lamps, and posters tacked to the unfinished homasote walls. What Hugh wanted was to destroy the past, remake it in his own image.

Phyllis came up with Hugh every weekend, and while he started renovating, I was slowly preempted by her in the kitchen and the garden. When I complained to him, he agreed to have her up every other weekend and I'd have my friends up on alternate ones, but on those weekends he refused to speak to me. His silence was devastating. He and Phyllis didn't try to hide their active distaste for my friends. Eventually I let him buy me out.

Hugh got his revenge on our father by ultimately transforming his little clapboard cottage into Mad King Ludwig's hunting lodge. The living room ceiling was removed and the little cramped bedrooms upstairs became balconies, and the Homasote walls were covered with wood varnished a deep golden, every inch hand-done by him; carved columns, cornices, niches, and finials, gold-leafed words up the side of the stairs: "I cannot know how far I can go until I go as far as I can." The exposed beams were hung with tassels, flags, and velvet draperies. He was a discerning flea market shopper, and assorted animal skulls, putti, plaster busts, and death masks encrusted the walls. It took him years, but he completely effaced the place I loved.

We eventually agreed to split the property in half: he got the lower part with the house, and I got the wooded lot in back, on which I eventually built a house.

Oklahoma! Tour

THAT SUMMER OF 1964 I WAS TOURING IN A SUMMER STOCK PRO-duction of *Oklahoma!* starring John Raitt as Curley. I played Ado Annie. Most of the leads had made careers of their roles. The Laurey had played her part so many times she was a blank-eyed automaton in rehearsals, boasting of the twenty meat loaves she had made and frozen for her family back home. Aunt Eller also displayed a plastic heartiness, and the Hakim character was a dentist who took summers off every year to play the part with all the skill of a dentist. This shocked me. I was fresh off my first Broadway show. What was I doing here? On top of this, the guy playing Will Parker opposite me took an instant dislike to me. In rehearsals he would refuse to work with me on the grounds that I was upstaging him, which was impossible because we were playing in the round. On the other hand, I probably was playing all by myself. I didn't give a hoot about his lasso tricks.

Alfred Cibelli, "Chibbie" had played Judd in all of Raitt's tours over the years, but his lack of freshness was less obvious because he wasn't obliged to be cheery. Later on I discovered he was incapable of cheery. He really was as morose as Judd. Possibly more.

We were playing the Melody Fair tent in North Tonawanda, New York. The motel where we were put up was in the middle of an abysmal wasteland of stubbly fields and abandoned factories. There was no place to hang out besides the restaurant, the swimming pool, and—for laughs—the gift shop, which sold plastic Indians, canoes, and toilet ashtrays.

I was very lonely. Chibbie also seemed to be alone, sunning himself by the swimming pool day after day. He was exotically handsome, dark-skinned with burning blue eyes and a Quixote beard. He looked like an El Greco—not at all my type. But we had both gotten bad reviews in the North Tonawanda paper: his Judd was too mean and my Ado Annie was too nymphomaniacal. I approached him with this bit of shared fate. He was passively available. I just grabbed hold and held on.

1964: Bad Times

CHIBBIE AND I HAD A DATE TO MEET AT MY APARTMENT AFTER WE got back to New York. When he didn't show up I fell apart. I had no idea he was living with a girlfriend. I was still smarting from being treated as if I didn't exist by my previous lover and my brother. I started drinking vodka gimlets and swallowing the painkillers I had for my teeth, which were beginning their long process of falling out. I only wanted to kill the pain I was in, not myself. I woke up in intensive care at St. Vincent's Hospital. Somebody was laughing. Deep, gut-busting laughing, coming from the nurse sitting at the foot of my bed. It must have been something the other nurse said. But I started laughing, too, and when the nurse saw this corpse with tubes up her nose laughing, she laughed even harder.

I was probably still a little high, but life seemed wonderful to me. I was detained by law for two weeks. Chib came to see me in the hospital. I don't know how he found out what I had done but I suspect he saw himself as the cause. The psychiatrist there informed me that Chibbie was a "bum" and that suicide was a sin. I refused to see this jerk again. While I was there I saw these other shaky, defenseless souls—I think now they were mostly alcoholics—who were being given spinals. Some of them said it made them violently ill. Early one morning, a nurse woke me up and took me to have a spinal, and I wept so noisily they let me go. Later a social worker sidled up to me in the hall and whispered,

"Miss Wilson, you don't have to have a spinal if you don't want to." The final stupidity was releasing me with a big bottle of Thorazine. The pills that got me in there in the first place weren't yet out of my system. I began to nod off while standing up in the street. When I mentioned the Thorazine to my regular doctor, he threw a penlight at the wall. It had given me what he called a "low-grade kidney infection." Once I stopped taking them I got my energy back and went looking for a new apartment.

Phyllis had an apartment on West 12th Street. She knew a man who could see from the back of his brownstone in the next block that the apartment in the building next to hers was empty. The rent was $175 a month, shockingly low even back then. It was what was called a "parlor floor-through," two big high-ceilinged rooms with marble fireplaces and back windows overlooking a garden. Soon after I moved in, Chibbie left his girlfriend and joined me.

1965: *Flora the Red Menace*

*J*UST AROUND THE TIME I WAS RECOVERING, JANE CONNELL CALLED me about a role in this new musical she had just read for, *Flora the Red Menace*, she said I was perfect for it, that I should audition. Nobody does this kind of thing; nobody calls up another actor to recommend a role they're up for themselves. Jane was a rare bird, a truly good soul devoid of malice. Her mate, Gordon, was the same. Gordon and I worked on songs and in shows together for over thirty years.

This role was Ada, a stiff, humorless Communist and Best Friend to the Star. I was indeed perfect for it, and I got the part. This was John Kander and Fred Ebb's first Broadway musical. George Abbott was the director: tall, intimidating, and, at 77, a living legend. Mr. Abbott didn't like to work with stars. The role of Flora was given to nineteen-year-old newcomer Liza Minnelli. One day early on, Liza said to me, "We have to get together! Get a hamburger or something!" We never did.

She was soon so distracted that when we passed each other backstage, she didn't seem to know who I was. She was a wild-eyed colt.

Mr. Abbott didn't like double names. He called me "Marylouisamayallcott." Mr. Abbott ruled absolutely. There was no dissension in the ranks, no behind-the-scenes skullduggery. The actors were shocked that he gave them line readings. Apparently when somebody once asked him, "What's my motivation?" he replied, "Your paycheck." I got it that musicals have abbreviated narratives and giving line readings was his way of working in shorthand. One day in New Haven, he came down the aisle chortling, and said to John and Fred, "I've got a grand idea!" In the first act, Ada had a scene with a character called the Cowboy. Then in the second act there was a scene with Liza sitting on a park bench while other characters made crossovers behind her. When the Cowboy crossed over and Liza said hello, he said "Howdy." Then I crossed the other way, Liza said hello and I said hello. Mr. Abbott's "grand idea" was that I would say "Howdy" instead. John and Fred were mystified. That night, the Cowboy said "Howdy" and crossed over, then I came the opposite way, said "Howdy," and the audience exploded. From that one word they knew Ada had fallen for the Cowboy.

Mr. Abbott was brutal with me. I had a big number, "The Flame," and he had a big whistle. We were trying out the show in New Haven. I stood there stiff as a board singing the song, and he blew that goddammed whistle at me again and again. He yelled at me and I had no clue what he wanted me to do. I wasn't "taking stage," but I didn't know that. I was still telling myself, Just stand there, don't do anything to destroy the laugh. I went back to my crummy room in the Taft Hotel. The walls were paper thin; every night I sat in the tub with the faucets thundering and wailed my heart out.

Something else that made matters worse was my rocky romance with Chibbie. He came up to visit me in New Haven, and the first time Mr. Abbott laid eyes on him he glared holes through him. Mr. Abbott would have objected to any kind of distracting liaison, but in this case he was personally infuriated because, as I found out later, Chibbie had at one time married a girlfriend of Mr. Abbott's. Chib was fifteen years older than me and had three former wives. Now in New Haven he was behaving badly, throwing chairs and threatening to leave me. I was afraid he would walk out. In the midst of a yelling match, I suggested we get married. When the show got to Boston, we went before a justice of the peace. The minute the man said, "I now pronounce you man and wife," I felt iron gates slam shut behind me. I knew it was a mistake, but I went ahead with it anyway.

Mr. Abbot, famous for pinching pennies, travelled on the bus with the cast to New York. He got wind of the marriage just as we boarded, and all the way down to New York he fulminated on the evils of smoking, drinking, and marriage. He was no celibate; Mr. Abbott was in splendid condition, and there were tales of his chasing young things around his hotel suite.

I had my own private hells. There were high notes in "The Flame" that made my throat raw. I was hyperventilating at the dinner table with my mistaken husband, and I had such a bad case of hemorrhoids that, two nights before we opened, I went to a doctor. With my ass upended on the table, the doctor leaned down to my face and asked, "Can you get me two tickets for opening night?"

Flora opened to mixed reviews. Mr. Abbott came around and apologized to the cast for not realizing that, in the Cold War, the audience wasn't ready to accept New York Communists. Liza won a Tony anyway. And Mr. Abbott turned to me and said, "Ada? You're great." The cast sent him a gift for his 78th birthday and in return we got typed thank-you notes. Written in ink across the bottom of mine: "You're a grand actress." Maybe everybody got a line like that, but after what he put me through, I cherished mine.

1960s-1970s: Industrial Shows

*I*NDUSTRIALS WERE EARLY MORNING BREAKFAST SHOWS HELD IN hotel ballrooms. They were live commercials put on for the trade. They became a hot ticket for people from our business when clever writers like Marshall Barer, Burt Shevelove, and Ronny Graham began writing for them. They wrote funny lyrics about shirts and polyester and gas to well-known Broadway tunes. In the Men's Sportsman Show, Larry Kert, the star of *West Side Story* sang to the tune of "Maria": "Banana, the color this year is banana . . ."

For a while there in the late sixties, I was the Industrial Queen. The Men's Sportswear Show cast was comprised of young, good-looking Broadway singers and dancers, a couple of seasoned funny men, and myself, the lone female. The first show I did, I walked into the rehearsal room and ten chairs scraped back and ten gorgeous men stood up to greet me. We did a number to the tune of "The Continental," and I was dancing with these guys, being tossed hither and yon, swaying and kicking. I felt like Ginger Rogers. I loved it. The comedy-sketch guys, George Irving, a gentle bear with a deep basso, and Morty Marshall, a pint-size, grizzled-voiced misanthrope, were my sketchmates, both very funny men. And they let me be funny, too.

This was all going on at seven in the morning. We had to be at the hotel by six to get ready. Once I was sitting in the backstage area pasting a fake diamond in my navel for a belly-dance number while having a conversation about which was better, Greenwich Village or the Upper West Side, and I suddenly thought, If I can do this—get up this early and have an argument while pasting a diamond in my navel—I must belong in show business.

One year, Ronny Graham wrote and performed in the Men's Sportswear Show. Ronny was a dark, skinny, deeply funny guy with a permanent five o'clock shadow and a hipster manner. He was funny just standing there. To the tune of "Money" from *Cabaret*, a chorus of guys sang "leather, leather, leather, leather" while a hirsute Ronny came onstage in leather "hot pants," mesh hose, and high heels, flicking a toy whip at the business men at the front tables and hissing in a German accent, "Eat your eggs!" He also wrote dirty lyrics to the Peggy Lee song, "Is That All There Is?", which I sang wearing leather "hot pants."

The Milliken shows were lavish productions held in the ballroom at the Waldorf Astoria for five consecutive mornings. Milliken Mills was advertising polyester; the cast was costumed in permanent press and sang songs about no-iron wear. The shows had twenty "Beautiful Milliken Girls," big stars and famously huge bonuses. The first one I did starred Bert Lahr. The first day of rehearsals he walked in, picked up the script, and said to nobody in particular, "How many woids?" He treated the audience like faces painted on canvas. Each morning he appeared onstage with the twenty Beautiful Milliken Girls lined up behind him and hissed out of the corner of his mouth, "What's my line?" Twenty Beautiful Milliken girls murmured back, "Good morning." "Good morning!" he would bellow at the audience. "Good morning!"

The Milliken people decided I was their new darling and called to tell me they had written their next show around me. I was in previews for *Flora the Red Menace* and I couldn't imagine getting up at dawn to sing and then doing the same at night. I thought my lungs might fall out. I turned them down, once again guilt-ridden for not having the requisite chutzpah. They never forgave me. I was cast in subsequent shows, but in tiny roles. It felt like punishment. I didn't know producers took things so personally. Still, the bonuses were worth it; enough to build my house in the country.

The last industrial I did was a one-day job for Cy Martin, Clothier to the Stars, in the Royal Box at the Americana Hotel. Besides myself, this one starred a guy in a leprechaun suit, two Latin Quarter beauties, and Harry Lorayne, the "memory expert." One day, a few weeks after the show, I passed Harry on the street. I said, "Hi, Harry!" but he didn't remember me.

The Marriage

*M*Y PARENTS WERE TORN BETWEEN SHOCK AT MY CHOICE OF HUS-band and delight that I was finally married. They eventually got used to Chibbie and accepted him. Hugh and Taffy reacted with dismissive sniffs. Some of my snobbier friends made it obvious that they thought I had married beneath me. He and I didn't share the same tastes. I deplored his choice of menswear and bad oil paintings. But Chib was basically a sweet man, and lost, like me. At least I got some decent bed linens, and silverware out of it.

I thought being a married couple would make it easier to appear at social events. The agony of getting dressed up and arriving alone at a party was over, now that there were two of us. As things turned out, it took twice as long to get ready, and sometimes both of us ended up standing in the closet in tears.

The good thing about the marriage was that it allowed me to turn down jobs I didn't want with the excuse that I had to be with my husband. I was hiding. I spent most of the marriage watching Julia Child on television and cooking dishes like *choucroute garnie* and Beef Wellington in our vestigial kitchen. Sometimes Chib would cook innards or brains and the smell drove me out of the house. We had a fight once when I was in the middle of cooking a lamb navarin. I threw a bulb baster at him and then left to sit in the park and cool off. When I got back he had finished making the dish. We sat down and ate and it was delicious. We were pushing back out chairs when Maybelle my English bulldog started to retch. After a moment she threw up the herb bouquet.

Chib wouldn't allow Maybelle to sleep on the bed. Once he said, "You love that dog more than me!" I said of course I did. I didn't see anything odd about that. He didn't really love me any more than I him. We were both so moribund. We had nothing else in common. We lay side by side in bed like graven knights on their tombs, sneering at the television. "Look! That's a hairpiece! So obvious." "Her eyes have completely disappeared!" "He has the biggest schwanz in Hollywood."

Chibbie got cast as the Captain in *Man of La Mancha* when it opened in the Village in '65. I went to see the first preview and informed him that it was a bomb, it wouldn't last a week. It turned out to be a huge hit and I ended up accompanying members of his family as well as my own to see it, and watching in astonishment as tears dribbled down their cheeks. Our apartment was littered with figurines of Don Quixote and Sancho Panza. My absolute limit for staying in any show was eleven months, but Chib was one of those actors who stays with a show until it closes. *La Mancha* lasted five years. Longer than our marriage.

It wasn't all bad times, but after three years we agreed to end it. The depth of my sorrow surprised me. I had an overwhelming sense of failure.

Almost thirty years later, I was pinch-hitting for the vacationing actress playing Parthy in *Show Boat*. I passed the open door of Cap'n Andy's, i.e., John Cullum's, dressing room and saw him and the actor Jack Dabdoub, who played Vallon. They were chortling away about something. I asked what was so funny and Jack asked if I ever knew a character actor named Cibelli. I said yeah, I was married to him. They both looked like they'd been smacked. I asked, "Why? What's so funny?" "Oh," Jack said, "we were just remembering how gloomy he was, uh—I just came from his wake. Oh, that's my cue!" and rushed onstage.

I have no competitive sense, so I just went ahead. See, if you compete, you're looking left and right and it holds you back. I knew no one knew what I knew and I didn't question it. —D.V.

Auditioning

*I*N THE FIFTIES AND SIXTIES, AUDITIONS WERE HELD IN THEATERS. I was let in the stage door by an ancient doorman who gestured me to stand in a spot just offstage, jammed up against redolent old ropes and set pieces. My heart thumped in the hushed darkness. Then a smiling man with a clipboard approached and whispered, "Miss Wilson?" Then he walked onto the stage and announced my name. A moment, then he beckoned, and I walked out. I had my script. I couldn't see my executioners sitting out front. Disembodied voices greeted me from the dark, then asked me to read. Standing center stage in the single light, framed by the proscenium and enveloped by darkness on all sides, I immediately felt, I belong here. My voice feels right here. All my young life people have been telling me to lower it, but here I can be heard in the top balcony.

Sometime in the seventies, auditions began to be held in dance studios: big, airy rooms with sun pouring through the windows, mirrored walls, fluorescent lights, and booming acoustics. Down at one end was a long table where the firing squad sat. If it was for a play, I sort of wandered two thirds of the way down, almost within shooting distance. For a musical, floating roughly halfway down like a buoy was an upright piano. You swam to it. There was no place to hide. I didn't know what to do with my arms, where to put my eyes. Look right at them? Over their heads? Shut them? Now that I could see their eyes, I could see boredom, squirming, sleeping, even eating—lunch I suppose—as I attempted to shake their world. Hopeless.

Film interviews with people from L.A. who are in town for the weekend are often held in Midtown hotel rooms; I sit in a tiny room on a squishy sofa, knee to knee with the director while sinking helplessly into a semi-recumbent position. I've been told I won't have to read, the call is to "meet the director." It's a personality contest. I do my impersonation of a hip gal, then they give me a script and ask if I wouldn't mind reading a few lines. I step into the hall to look it over, then come back in. It's no use.

I've been auditioning for some fifty years now. You never get beyond it. Once you think of yourself as "known," the people who knew you have been replaced by younger people who've never heard of you.

I would rather eat bulls' balls than audition. I would rather be hung by the ankles in a public square. Upside down. In the nude.

The very thought of having to compete makes me want to lie down and die. I am filled with resentment that I have to prove myself over and over again. The first time I look at a part I'm sure I'm not right for it. If the character is "wealthy and aristocratic" I'm too scruffy, I don't have the fingernails for it, not to mention the earrings. If she's an Okie, "poor and shabby," I'm too refined. "Homely?" Too attractive. "Kindly?" Hard as rocks. But then who the hell am I? I have no idea.

Getting ready, I drag everything I own out of the closet and try it all on, attempting to find the character in the clothes. The room is festooned with discarded outfits, I crash around in one shoe moaning, banging my head with a hairbrush, wishing me like to one more rich in hope. I end up doing everything but studying the script.

It didn't occur to me that I should put any extra muscle into a reading, that I should try to perform. My attitude was, I will simply read the lines and let them see what potential I have. How could I be expected to do more when I don't know the script? When they didn't respond, I was stunned. Silence followed by "Thank you," then out onto the street. This happened so many times I became convinced I had lost my talent.

Singing

*I*N THE NORMAL PROCESS OF LEARNING LINES, ONCE YOU'VE LEARNED them they sink into some subterranean cave below conscious memory. You don't try to think of a line while performing any more than you think about your feet while jumping rope. But if I lose my concentration and go blank in a play, at least I can take a pause or two or four, or improvise. When I'm singing, there's something about just knowing I can't stop that can cause me to crash and burn. I have a lifelong affliction of going blank on song lyrics. The music is a speeding train coming toward me and I'm tied to the tracks. A full orchestra is racing over me and the more important the occasion, like opening nights, the critics or the President out front, the stronger the likelihood of me causing everything to come to a screeching halt. This is why I beg people not to say who's out there. It could be your great aunt Mabel, but if I thought of her, I would go down.

I had no desire to be a singer, but it seemed that in order to be funny a person had to sing. And dance! No. I don't dance. At least, not in public. Alone in my living room with "Light My Fire" on the radio, I can swivel my hips with the best of them. But the moment a choreographer looks at my feet and says, "a one, and a two, and a three," I'm a dead person. I'm back in algebra class.

The usual call for singing auditions was a ballad and an "up-tune." The up-tune was to see if you could carry a beat. I couldn't swing and click my fingers. It would be like asking Buster Keaton to smile, which I believe the poor guy was once forced to do, years after his film fame, when he was playing the mute King in a national tour of *Once Upon a Mattress*, and the photographer taking a cast photo yelled: "Hey you! Yeah, you with the hat! Give us a smile!"

I didn't sing at musical auditions, I shouted. And I couldn't shout in the song's original key, somebody had to transpose it down a few feet. There were accompanists who could transpose on sight and those who couldn't, and sometimes I didn't know who was which until it was too late and disaster ensued. I eventually learned to bring my own accompanist. One of my first accompanists was a tall, pimply teenager named Marvin Hamlisch. He was working his way through college playing piano. And he played piano like a fourteen-piece orchestra. I was in his family's apartment practicing a song one day and his mother came into the room wailing, "Marvin! Please! Eat a little!" It was like a Clifford Odets play. Marvin soon graduated to bigger things.

Wally Harper

WITH THE ADVENT OF JONI MITCHELL AND CAROLE KING, auditions called for songs with a rock beat. The only pianist I knew who could play a rock beat was Wally Harper. When I asked him to play for me, he said, "Mary Louise, do you know why people laugh when you sing?" I didn't know people were laughing. I was torn between being offended and pleased, I'm so craven for laughs. He said, "Because you forget to breathe!" He refused to play for me but he offered to teach me how to sing.

Wally Harper, skinny, bucktoothed, brilliant Wally, was the creator and other half of Barbara Cook's singing act. They were just beginning to put it together when I began working with him.

Wally gave me a voice. He would straddle the piano bench and hold down my uvula—a dangling piece of flesh that hangs in the back of the throat, dear reader—and give me a note, and slowly he stretched my vocal cords until one day a note popped out that sounded like an adolescent boy's. My range began to expand. He gave me a head voice; some decent sounds between middle and high C.

Wally was a musical genius: behind closed doors, alone with him at the piano, I lost my inhibition. He got me to sing with real feeling. One day he persuaded me to sing in front of some friends. I clutched. It didn't go well. I was like the frog in that famous cartoon: a man opens a box and a frog hops out singing and tap dancing. The man sees dollar signs. The frog is reciting Shakespeare and singing "Vesti la Giubbe" as the man is running to a talent agent with the box. When he gets to the agent he opens the box, the frog jumps out, goes down on all fours and croaks.

1991: A Reading at Playwrights Horizons

W E HAD SENT A COPY OF *FULL GALLOP* TO THE PLAYWRIGHTS Horizons Theater, and out of the blue one day, the then dramaturg, Tim Sanford, called us. He said he thought there was something interesting about our play and offered to give us a reading. We were thrilled. I was sure this would lead directly to a full New York production.

Until now, I hadn't realized the importance of Mrs. Vreeland's seating arrangement. For the Playwright's reading, I was given one of those cantilevered metal chairs you see outside motel units that tilts you backward. I was peering over my knees to see the audience. The strain nearly killed me. Our audience turned out to be mostly friends and well-wishers, in spite of the huge mailing we sent out.

André Bishop

T HE READING TOOK PLACE ON THE SAME DAY THAT ANDRÉ BISHOP, then head of Playwrights, was leaving to take over as Artistic Director of Lincoln Center Theater. On top of this, during the reading I developed a massive toothache in a back molar, which was extracted the next morning. I already had a dental history with André: I was in *Sister Mary Ignatius Explains It All For You* at Playwrights, and then *Baby With the Bathwater,* and I told him I had to leave *Bathwater* because my front tooth was falling out. I have a memory of this gentle, soft-spoken man peering solicitously into my mouth. I was too embarrassed to mention that my dentist, a coke addict recommended to me by my friend Pamela Reed, had stuck my temporaries in with Crazy Glue and that it wasn't working.

I don't know if André saw the reading, but we got a call a few days later inviting us to meet with him in his Lincoln Center office. He told us he didn't know how much general interest there was in the world of fashion, but he offered to introduce us to a friend of his who belonged to the Cosmopolitan Club, a prestigious women's organization. Former members included Eleanor Roosevelt and Helen Hayes.

Television Commercials

*A*FTER *FLORA THE RED MENACE*, I WASN'T GOING DOWN, BUT I wasn't going up either. I was going on commercial auditions.

For the better part of the sixties and seventies, I traipsed up and down Madison Avenue. I told myself that it was underwriting my stage career, but it felt like my main occupation. I went on an average of fifteen auditions for every commercial I got. Some actors were getting very rich from them. Sitting in the waiting rooms, I heard about the number of spots they had made that were "in the can." They chatted away about their farms in Bucks County, their children's enrollment at L'Ecole Française, and their private planes.

One big irritation was the clothes. I thought one of the best things about being in the theatre, besides not having to take the subway during rush hour, was that I wouldn't ever have to wear office clothes again. I could wear jeans and sneakers in real life, and don gowns, cocktail hats, boas, and farthingales on stage, playing countesses, spies, and madwomen. The trouble was that the characters on commercials were "real" people. I had to put my office outfits back on again. And of course to get to an audition, I had to ride the subway at rush hour because the calls were invariably at nine Monday morning or five Friday afternoon.

Brigitte Bardot's lips made Mick Jagger's possible.
                                                    —*D.V.*

T HEN THERE WAS THE BUSINESS OF MAKEUP AND HAIR. UNTIL the sixties, the only makeup respectable women wore was lipstick. Lipstick was mandatory; you couldn't leave the house without lipstick, along with the cone bra that didn't show your nipples and the girdle that made a board of your bum. Men would actually become indignant if they noticed your lipstick had worn off, which is probably why lipstick back then was the texture of road tar. You could use face powder, because God forbid you should have a shiny nose, but that was all. Even Mrs. Vreeland wore only lipstick in those days. Then the sixties exploded, and suddenly the fashion was Cleopatra eye makeup and false eyelashes. I put on makeup for the show at night, but street makeup hadn't been perfected yet, and applying No. 6 Max Factor base and rouge to go to auditions in the light of day made me look like a fifty-year-old prostitute.

In the seventies it got so you couldn't go to the corner grocery without your false eyelashes. My struggles with gluing the goddamned things on usually reduced me to a sobbing wreck. By the time I finally had it down, they were out of fashion.

In the 1970s, the cry from casting offices heard 'round the world was, "What about her hair?" The requisite hairdo had become the bouffant. Or the bubble. Around this time, Vreeland began to be more visible to the outside world. She had worn her hair pulled back in a little snood until she, along with Jackie Kennedy, went to Paris and had their hair bouffant-ed by the famous hairdresser, Alexandre de Paris. Immediately everybody had to have the bouffant. There could be no wrinkles or dips in your hair, no strays, it had to be a lacquered dome. Like the hood of a car. Women with naturally kinky hair were having it ironed. When I wasn't sleeping with anybody, I went to bed with toilet paper wrapped around my head.

Mrs. Vreeland stuck with this look forever after, even exaggerating the slight mound, the little hill at the top of the crown that was part of the bouffant. She had it regularly dyed black, so black it looked navy blue.

I attempted the bouffant at home by rolling my hair up on empty frozen orange-juice containers. In my struggle to pin it up, all the blood would rush out of my arms and I would have a breakdown. Even with an entire can of hairspray, your coif could be completely undone by the wind of an oncoming A train.

Things got surreal in the mid seventies, when the hippie revolution finally reached Madison Avenue. Ad executives were wearing jeans, beads, and long hair and the receptionist with her tie-dye and flowing locks looked like La Belle Dame Sans Merci. The waiting room was designed like a "pad," and instead of sofas there were low poufs on which we actors in our Republican getups attempted to maintain a purchase.

Some auditions called for you to make a headache face. Or to burble like a coffee percolater. At one audition I was asked to laugh. Laugh at what? Nothing, just laugh. Make a big fool of yourself.

When I did get a job, the first thing was a call from the wardrobe department asking if I could bring in a housedress. Never mind that at this point housewives all over America were wearing jeans. A housedress? I was a New Yorker, for God's sake! Everything in my closet was black!

The call was for 6 a.m. I came into a space the size of an airplane hangar and a crew guy sitting on a wooden box sipping coffee said, "You Talent? See Makeup, then Hair." Makeup, an anorexic gentleman with dyed black hair and a buzz saw voice was smoking and coughing and yakking and cackling with Hair, a plump, surly woman wearing what looked like an orange fright wig. Without ceasing to yak, smoke, cackle, and cough his lungs up, Makeup motioned me to a chair, threw a plastic sheet over me, and started to jab and punch at my face with a sponge. He held my head in an arm grip as he applied mascara. My eyes kept watering. "Keep your lid up!" he yelled. "I can't!" I yelled back. He sniffed, sniggered to Hair, "Get a load of this one." At last he said, "Ok, you're done."

I looked in the mirror, and I couldn't believe what I was seeing. I was a nice-looking woman when I came in, now my eyebrows looked like Groucho's and my mouth was nowhere near the lipstick. I said, "Would you mind if I re-do my lips?"

"Can you believe this?" he shouted. "Can you believe the balls on this one?" His voice followed me down the hall. "She's got some balls on her, that one."

Actors were getting ill from having to eat Sara Lee cheesecake or drinking Vicks cough syrup over and over, thus the introduction of the "spit bucket." Heights of tables and chairs were adjusted for camera angles, which meant sometimes I was obliged to squat for great lengths of time next to a washing machine, looking perky and delivering lines. Lines were spoken while moving the product, say a bottle of Listerine, to invisible marks in space, and walking to various tape marks on the floor without looking down. In between takes, people rushed in to stir up soap suds, squirt glycerin on spaghetti or spray a wayward hair on my stiff head. On the breaks there was no place to sit. A row of agency "suits," happy to be out of the office, lounged in all the available chairs. The actor was the prop, the product was the star.

I ingested busloads of words by sheer force of will: "Vicks vaporizing cough syrup is a non-enteronically, alcalizing, fast-acting, germ-eradicating, doctor-tested cold medicine." I was great at rattling them off, but if it wasn't "in the can" before lunch, it was impossible for me to retain the words afterwards, and the rest of the afternoon was spent doing take after take after take.

At first only comedy actors did commercials. "Serious actors" wouldn't lower themselves until they copped to the money. In the end, even Orson Welles was hawking beer and Sir Laurence Olivier, Polaroid. Every time a commercial aired you got a residual check. I didn't make nearly as many commercials as others, but I still earned enough to install a Vicks VapoRub septic tank, dig a Cheer detergent well, and build an Excedrin deck for my house in Connecticut.

Unemployment

*T*HERE WERE MANY TIMES WHEN I WAS CONVINCED MY STAGE career was over and that I needed to find some other kind of work, but there was nothing else I was any good at. In one long fallow period, I decided I would go into the landscaping business. I worked with an insane Frenchman planting ornamental evergreens in the pouring rain and mud. Another time I thought I might teach acting at the local college, SUNY New Paltz, and I went to an interview with the head of the drama department. He effectively prevented me from submitting my résumé by giving me his critiques of current Broadway plays, pelting me with names like Betty Buckley and Patti LuPone while sitting at a desk in a small clearing of a jungle of men's suits and coats; apparently the men's costume department.

I spent a year in a writing course at Columbia University. The professor encouraged my writing, but when he announced to the class one day, "You can't do it alone!" I was daunted. On another seemingly interminable hiatus, in a moment of incipient hysteria I walked into a secretarial hiring office and tried to talk to the lady behind the desk, explaining in low, modest terms that I was an actress, but I had been a secretary before that and now would like to get back into that line of work. The lady didn't seem to hear me. It was as if I was air. I can't explain it. I think I must have been whispering. I drifted out the door.

Unemployment Insurance

THE LAST TIME I HAD THE TEMERITY TO COLLECT AN UNEMPLOY-
ment check was in 1984. I was able to register near my house upstate, I only had to go into the office once, and the rest of the time the
checks were mailed to me. As it happened, the one time I had to show
up at the office I was in the city the night before. I got up at dawn the
next day, put the cat in the car along with a thermos of coffee, and took
off. Halfway up the parkway, I started to open the thermos and lost control of the car. We did a U-turn and ended up in the middle of the road
facing oncoming traffic. Thank God at that hour there wasn't any, but
I got out with my cat and stood on the curb, hysterical. A surly cop
emerged out of nowhere, stood there while I turned the car around,
and gave me a $100 ticket. However, this brush with mortality galva-
nized me to go home and write about actors and unemployment, which
eventually turned into an article published in the Arts & Leisure section
of *The New York Times*.

The first time I collected unemployment insurance was in 1957,
and it was a weekly trip to Dante's Inferno. The office was a whole
floor of a building on Rector Street. We called it "Rectal Street" because when you walked in you were assailed by the odor of diarrhea.
The grim-faced staff displayed the attitude that anybody who was
unemployed was ipso facto a bum. In the fifties, waves of Puerto Ri-
cans were arriving in the city and looking for work, and the staff had
no knowledge of Spanish and no idea how to deal with them. Lines
led up to the counter where you signed for your weekly check. When
you finally got up there, the lady behind the counter barked, "Did you
work last week?" "No." "Are you ready to work?" "Yes." "Are you
willing to work?" "Yes." "Are you able to work?" "Yes." I was terrified
that they would make me take an office job. I had just escaped from
office jobs.

If you missed your assigned day or time to report, you were sent to Section B. You didn't want to go to Section B. You could be sent to Section B for no reason you knew and sit there all afternoon. Low moans came from Section B. Patricia Brooks, a beautiful soprano I knew who was eight months pregnant, was sent to Section B. After an hour she stood up and announced, "You think I'm not able to work?" then threw her head back and let out a gorgeous High C.

The Call

*I*T SEEMS TO BE A GIVEN THAT THE CALL FOR A JOB ONLY COMES after you've surrendered and bought a one-way ticket to Paris or enrolled in medical school. It seems as if it always must interfere with something else. With what, I ask myself? Isn't acting my life? But what is that other stuff called, those long stretches in between? When an actor's working, you're told where to be at what time, what to wear, what to say, and who you are. Then when the show's over you're suddenly stripped of all these directives. No reason to get out of bed. I once told Mac Dixon I thought the most important thing an actor can have to survive was a low rent. Mac disagreed. He said the most important thing is having something else you love to do. I have a garden.

Don't wait around for anything, because it never comes to you. You go after it. Then it comes to you. —D.V.

*A*FTER EACH PERFORMANCE OF *FULL GALLOP*, WE WOULD GET A surge of new ideas and go back to working on the script. But there were long periods—months—when there was no prospect of a gig, and we spent all our time trying to peddle the play. This was one hell of an operation, believe me. Email didn't exist in the eighties. Computers were barely in use, and getting a script together was no minor feat. Mark knew how to use a computer, but they had incompatible systems. Sometimes whole pages disappeared with no hope of retrieval, and drafts and rewrites were impossible to keep track of. We went absolutely nuts. But Mark somehow always managed to turn out a crisp new copy with a nice cover to mail to each person. It was expensive and labor intensive and a huge distraction from writing. Not to mention deeply depressing. Those few times we got a response, we were told it had been handed over to somebody who, we knew, would put it at the bottom of a ten-foot stack of submitted scripts. So many alleys we went up were dead-ends. It hadn't occurred to me how little clout I would have, less than a stranger's.

We spent weeks, sometimes months, bereft of inspiration. We had staring contests. Then we went out and ate a lunch someplace that left us even more stupefied. But we kept on showing up. I often think if either one of us had called and said we couldn't make it that day, it all might have crumbled into dust.

The Cosmopolitan Club

OUR INTERVIEW WITH ANDRÉ BISHOP WAS IN JANUARY '92. THE following October, we were invited to do a reading in the dining room of the Cosmopolitan Club. Each time we had a date for a gig, it recharged us to do more work on the script. I was now off book. The reading was held in the ballroom. I was on a settee this time, certainly an improvement over the cantilevered lawn chair, but I was on a platform overlooking a sea of upturned faces. Again I felt the need to lean forward over the chasm between us. The response was respectable, apparently I was sufficient pre-dinner entertainment. George Dwight was there, along with Vreeland's disapproving grandson Alexander, who, I was told, left before it was over.

Around the same time I was granted an audience with Lucille Lortel, the owner of the Theater de Lys (renamed the Lucille Lortel Theatre after her death). I was instructed by the young man who opened her apartment door to shout, as Ms. Lortel was very deaf. I was seated in a chair facing her. Our knees were touching. I started to read and she stopped me: "Stop shouting!" she shouted. "I can hear you perfectly well." I ploughed on in a miserable monotone until the end. Out on the street afterwards, Mark and I quarreled. He was furious that I didn't do a better reading, but there was no way in that situation to perform, to do anything but muddle through.

W E ALSO FOUGHT OVER POSSIBLE PERFORMANCE VENUES I DREW the line at riverboats. I was not going to go down the Mississippi as a tourist attraction. Later, however, I did go up the Amazon performing the play on a Theatre Guild cruise. For me, Patricia Neal was the one bright light onboard. She sang for her supper by telling the story of her romance with Gary Cooper, her subsequent marriage to Roald Dahl, and the tragedies that befell her children. The story was riveting and she told it without a shred of self-pity. I've never met anybody so completely devoid of ill will. The sound cues from the show were all off. Not that any of it mattered. Standing in the reception line after the show as the elderly audience shuffled past, the repeated question was, "Why the rouge on your ears?" My stock answer, "Because her mother did it," finally withered into, "I haven't the faintest idea."

1969: Cincinnati

M Y WHOLE LIFE, I SEEMED TO HAVE BOYFRIENDS OF FOREIGN EX-traction. It wasn't a conscious decision. Maybe I wanted to throw it in my parents' face, they were so obvious about wanting me to find a nice-looking preppie from a "good" family, no matter how dumb or dull or drunk. Or maybe I just identified with the underdog.

Shortly after my marriage ended, I went out to the Cincinnati Playhouse for two months to play Lady Would-be in Ben Jonson's

Volpone. When I got off the plane in Cincinnati a young person handed me a padlock key to the place where I was to live. I thought, Oh God, they're putting me in a broom closet. We drove up to a little house down a few steps from the street and there was a padlock on the door. I opened it, stepped inside, and fell in love. Besides the bedroom, kitchen, and bath, there was a living room with a terrace that overlooked the Ohio River. I had without question the best digs in the company. I immediately threw a party for the cast. Eddie, a young black actor, stayed behind to help me clean up. He wouldn't leave. He was twenty-three, I was thirty-seven. He was funny and charming and smart, and for a short while we were very much in love. I had never had a lover like Eddie. I would have done anything for him. I bought him a motorcycle. He introduced me to soul music—the Four Tops, Roberta Flack, the Temptations—and he showed me how to move, to separate my pelvis from my upper body. Eddie lived in Chicago, but when the show was over, and even though I warned him "you can't live on love," he followed me to New York and moved in with me. We would be wildly happy together for a few days, and then he would fall into these terrible depressions. I thought it was because the black actors he had contacted in the city had no desire to help a brother get work.

And then I got pregnant. This was 1969, shortly before abortion became legal. I knew women who had gone to this clinic in Puerto Rico. But I went to my GP, who, though I didn't realize it at the time, was insane. It's important to understand how a lot of doctors treated young unmarried women in those days. When a girl went to a gynecologist to be fitted for a diaphragm, it was common for him to ask how many men she had slept with. And I knew more than one girl who had been unnecessarily fondled while on the examination table, but said nothing through sheer intimidation.

I had been going to this guy for regular checkups ever since I came to the city. He had a proprietary attitude toward me, which I interpreted as protective. Being the daughter of a doctor and instilled with the belief that they were gods, I never questioned his attentions. Each time he examined my nether regions, he would exclaim, "My God, you should be married!" I would stop by for a B12 shot on the way to a rehearsal, and as I dashed out the door he'd say, "Got a minute for me to check your unnms?" while make squeezing motions with his hands. I viewed it as physicianly concern.

So I listened when he told me I couldn't have the child because I was thirty-seven and the child would be retarded. I knew I shouldn't have it, but he robbed me of making that choice. He didn't want me to go to "some filthy, dirty clinic" in Puerto Rico either. He would arrange for me "a clean, safe abortion right here in the city." Then he asked how much I could pay. I had about a thousand dollars in savings. He gave me the name of a doctor who would do it, a Park Avenue gynecologist. When I called him, he told me to meet him on the corner of Madison Avenue and 54th Street and bring a thousand dollars in cash. I saw a black Cadillac idling at the curb. The door opened, a hand gestured, I got in. The doctor was wearing dark glasses. I gave him the cash. I was in a low-budget mafia movie.

The whole experience was something out of a Fellini nightmare. It took place in a building just off Madison in the 60s, around the corner from fashionable art galleries. It wasn't exactly a hospital. A woman, not a nurse, handed me a jelly glass saying, "Pee-pee in this," and pointed to what looked like a broom closet. It was indeed a broom closet, with a toilet in it; once seated it wasn't possible to completely close the door. The room I was assigned to wasn't much bigger. It had two beds jammed so close together only one person at a time could get in or out. Fortunately or not, the woman in the other bed didn't move. She could have been dead for all I knew.

The operation was to take place the next morning. I couldn't sleep, I read *Portnoy's Complaint* from cover to cover. Somewhere in the middle of the night, a man with a bad toupee and a paper sunflower sticking out of the pocket of his green surgeon's shirt came in and winking broadly asked if I was "Mrs. Wilson." Maybe they thought by this time any sane woman would have fled the place. The next morning, as I was wheeled into the operating room, I noticed paint peeling off the ceiling. As I went under, I heard the doctors laughing loudly about something. The rest of that day I cried. I cried myself to sleep that night. I wasn't prepared for the grief that swallowed me.

A week later, an actress friend told me she had just had an abortion in Puerto Rico. The clinic was spanking clean, she paid $500 by check, she had the operation the day she flew in and flew back that night without removing her false eyelashes.

When I came home from the hospital, I found lying on the desk these photographs of two black women. I looked closely: one was Eddie's girlfriend from Chicago who must have come to visit, and the other was Eddie. He admitted his compulsion to dress up. It was a terrific shock, but I felt pity for him. I loved him. I took him shopping, helped him find dresses and a wig and makeup and canoe-size high heels. Helping him dress was exhausting. He ended up looking like the Seagram Building while I looked like his charlady. He was a cute guy, but a really ugly woman. And boring. She was a completely different personality.

After a while, dressing up wasn't enough; Eddie wanted to go out with me in public. I couldn't do that. I absolutely refused, but he said if I loved him I would do it. I relented. This was the era of the maxi coat, boots, and false eyelashes. We got all dolled up, me and my gigantic girlfriend, and went up to West 57th Street to see Visconti's *The Damned*, a film showing Nazi officers dressing up in women's panties and garter belts. I was in a state of terror. Surely people noticed this giantess in the wig standing next to me. I was certain we were going to run into Hal Prince or Dick Cavett. We didn't, but I refused to go out with him/her again. Still, my heart ached for him.

We were together for about a year. Toward the end, Eddie got a job at Macy's for the Christmas holidays, and then spent most of his salary on an aquarium for me. The last thing I needed: fish, fish food, net, pump.

God. A few months later he left me for some other woman snarling, "I can't make you happy!" No, he couldn't. When he left, Hugh came over from next door and in a rare gesture put his arms around me. He said I should cut the boy's heart out and keep it in the fish tank.

*I*N THE SEVENTIES I OFTEN SAW PHOTOGRAPHS OF MRS. VREELAND living it up at Studio 54 with Andy Warhol and Candy Darling. I read about her in 1971 when she was fired from *Vogue*, and then again in '73, when she took a job at the Costume Institute of the Metropolitan Museum. She was later quoted as saying, "I was only 70. What was I supposed to do, retire?"

The website Diana Vreeland.com on her work at the Met:

At that time [the Costume Institute] could best be described as "sleepy," and Mrs. Vreeland immediately redefined its historically correct, yet lackluster, curatorial style. In the galleries of the Met, she was free to create an entire fantasy world, rather than be confined by two-dimensional magazine spreads. For her exhibitions she incorporated music, lighting design, props, even fragrances. She transformed mannequins from mere dummies into characters acting out dramatic scenes. Mrs. Vreeland refused to compromise her artistic vision for historical accuracy, controversially pairing pieces from different time periods and reworking garments to fit within her overall mise-en-scène. For this she drew criticism from scholars, yet simultaneously created unprecedented surges in attendance, galvanized countless new benefactors, and completely revitalized the Costume Institute.

Mrs. Vreeland's exhibitions became sources of inspiration for contemporary audiences—rather than simply presenting the exquisite costumes of the Ballets Russes or wardrobe from Hollywood films, they became "celebrations" of history. The fourteen shows she mounted ran the gamut from high-fashion designers like Balenciaga and YSL to exotic attire from China's Ch'ing Dynasty and Hapsburg Austria-Hungary.

Though she remained at the Met until her death in 1989, her greatest contributions surpassed its walls, for she truly shifted the way the world looked at fashion. Mrs. Vreeland introduced the public and press to "fashion as high art"—the idea that garments are just as much masterworks as paintings or sculpture. Furthermore, that the fashion of an era possesses a cultural and historic gravitas that should be studied and immortalized. Seeing the immense popularity of the Vreeland shows, Costume Institutes the world over revamped their own curatorial styles. Without the precedent Mrs. Vreeland set, shows such as Alexander McQueen: Savage Beauty at the Met and Madame Grès: La Coutur À L'œuvre at Musée Bourdelle in Paris, among myriad others, would never have been brought to light.

I adore artifice! —D.V.

VREELAND MADE A LOT OF COSTUME PRESERVATIONISTS FURIOUS by making new gowns for eighteenth-century models, even cross-pollinating eras. She would not have allowed Leonardo's "Last Supper" crumbling to dust on the convent wall in Milan to be shown without a complete makeover.

I went to her Hollywood exhibit: Joan Crawford, Bette Davis, Olivia de Havilland, and Joan Fontaine in gorgeous gowns by Adrian and Edith Head. Her voice on the little tape machine describing what I was seeing was in itself a great treat.

The story goes that during work on her last exhibit on India, she was blind and confined to her bed, so she had friends like designer Bill Blass check things out for her and report back. He told her that there was something "off" about the models in their saris—something inauthentic. She mulled this over, then telephoned the workers and ordered them to cut all the dress models in half and remove about three inches from their middles. They were put back together and then they looked right—they looked like the Indian woman.

*I have astigmatism like El Greco. I see girls and I see the
way their feet fall off the sidewalk when they're getting
ready to cross the street but they're waiting for the light,
with their marvelous hair blowing and their fatigued
eyes.* —D.V.

Full Gallop

W E WERE LOOKING UNDER ROCKS FOR PEOPLE TO TAKE AN
interest in our script. We sent *Full Gallop* to theater owners,
literary agents, anybody who had known Vreeland, and everyone else
we could think of. We heard about this play-reading group at Lincoln
Center under the aegis of John Guare. I was friendly with John, we ran
into each other in the Village all the time, so I dropped the script off
with a note at his apartment. One day, months later, I bumped into him
and he spluttered, "Mark Hampton the designer's a friend of mine! I
didn't know he was a playwright!" There was indeed the designer Mark
Hampton. There is also the Native American film actor Graham
Greene, but I would not in a million years mistake him for the Graham
Greene who wrote *The Heart of the Matter*.

Sybil Christopher had been very cordial to me when I shared a
dressing room with her daughter Kate Burton when she was making her
Broadway debut as Alice in *Alice in Wonderland* in the late seventies. I
called her about considering the script for her Bay Street Theatre. It
was a very odd conversation—well, not a conversation at all, as she
fended off all inquiries by launching into a diatribe having to do with
stopping smoking that so defied interruption I eventually hung up.

We sent the script to the director Mark Lamos, who ran the Hartford Stage. I had just worked with him. I heard nothing from him until
months later, in another chance encounter, I mentioned the script to
him. He opened his mouth wide, inhaled deeply and shouted, "I
LUHUHUHOST IT!"

We sent it to Lynn Meadow at the Manhattan Theatre Club and received a note thanking us, but informing us that MTC didn't do monologues. I even pressed the script onto my pal Nicky Martin, and watched as he let it slide out of his hand onto the floor.

The fact is, if you never want to hear from somebody again, send them your play. I confess that I myself have been sent plays I didn't ask for, and I know what it feels like; you resent the obligation. Still, our script was positively anemic compared to some of the phone books I've received over the years—deadly opuses with cover letters from the playwright saying they had me especially in mind for the lead, which was usually a backwoods hag with herbal powers or an angry, gin-swilling ex-cop with cancer. I imagined the playwright in his garret scribbling away and thinking, "Gee, this really stinks. This is perfect for Mary Louise Wilson."

You have to know somebody. And they have to need you. They have to have a hole in their schedule and a healthy budget, and then they might be interested. Whether the play is any good or not has little bearing here. As Mae West said to the little girl who exclaimed "My goodness!" when she saw her diamonds, "Goodness had nothing to do with it, dearie."

Several people rejected the script because it "lacked social significance." I was shocked to realize how hidebound, sentimental, and literal-minded the theater establishment could be. Why wasn't an evening in the company of a witty, worldly woman enough?

We sent the script to the talent agent I was with, who said he would pass it on to their literary department. Here's the letter the reader sent back:

This is not a play. This is a bunch of stories about things that happened to this lady who's talking that are not interesting to us. The audience can't relate. She talks about people we don't know, and about silly stuff, fashion, old times she had. There's no plot. Nothing happens. The character uses words that don't mean anything and repeats words. This is very poorly written.

If anything could have crushed us completely it would have been this. It was obviously written by some half-wit kid. But it was in keeping with the general contempt that I suffered at the hands of these people who were supposed to be representing me.

1972: *Gypsy*

ARTHUR LAURENTS WAS DIRECTING A NEW PRODUCTION OF *Gypsy* starring Angela Lansbury and he cast me as the stripper Tessie Tura. When I auditioned, I was asked to show my legs. I was delighted; they had never previously been required to audition. I couldn't have asked for a better musical to be in. *Gypsy* has everything: great story, thrilling music, and wonderful characters. I saw the original production with Ethel Merman. Even when we were rehearsing our version, I sensed Jerome Robbins's genius everywhere—in the tight script, the witty choreography, and the complete absence of sentimentality.

I was upset when Arthur kept me after school to rehearse. He said, "We don't want that Mary Louise Wilson stuff." What the hell was he talking about? I had great timing, I knew how to deliver lines like, "I don't do no scenes. Now go screw." Stephen Sondheim and Arthur were both at me for something more. They wanted Tessie to be prissy and affected. Arthur demonstrated by mincing around the rehearsal room, waving his wrists. I felt harassed and resentful, but I imitated him, and eventually got it. It was a great character choice. I didn't feel underestimated by Arthur; on the contrary, he seemed a bit obsessed with me, enjoyed playing Svengali to my Trilby.

My costume was scanty and gorgeous with blue chiffon butterfly wings and a sequined butterfly flap that flipped smartly when I did my bumps. I wore a curly red wig and a headache band with quivering butterfly antennae, and I managed to go up on pointe in my high heels for at least two seconds.

We went on a six-month tour before coming to Broadway. By far the worst thing that could have happened occurred during the first week of rehearsals, when the young actress playing Miss Mazeppa, Jackie Britt, was killed in an elevator accident. She had gone downtown on the lunch break for a workman's compensation hearing. It seemed that in each of the two shows she was in prior to this one, she'd had some kind of stage accident. We weren't told what actually happened on this day, but Jackie was a high-strung girl and knowing how scared she was of Arthur and nervous about getting back late, we thought the elevator might have stalled and she panicked and tried to climb out. Sally Cooke who played Miss Electra, Denny Dillon who played Agnes, and I went to a coffee shop and sat there, stunned and weeping. As accustomed as I was to hanging out on my own, I bonded with them and we became buddies on the road.

Sally Cooke

SALLY COOKE HAD THE LOOKS OF A BIG DUMB BLONDE, BUT LURK-ing inside that voluptuous body, pale white skin, and baby voice was an eccentric polymath; she constantly surprised us with her knowledge of stagecraft, classical music, fine wines, and the Hebrew language, among other things. She was a master mechanic. You passed anything along the dressing room counter for her to fix, your eye pencil, your watch, and she lifted it up to her porcelain boobs, peered at it nearsightedly, fiddled with it with her long red nails, then passed it back down to you, fixed.

She was the only company member who travelled with a set of luggage rather than a steamer trunk. What she pulled out of those bags was flabbergasting. As we gathered at La Guardia for the start of the tour, she appeared in a hat and outfit—her recently deceased mother's clothes—that Princess Grace might have worn. She seemed to be fond of wearing other people's clothes. During rehearsals in Toronto, she wore Denny's chesterfield coat which, on her, was a three-quarter-length jacket. The rest of her getup was the same every day: jeans, yellow Mickey Mouse sweatshirt, and hair in tiny pigtails. Her sense of style seemed to have been formed by old Hollywood movies. On our day off, she lay on her bed in a gauzy black negligee and satin scuffs with marabou pom-poms, doing her nails and listening to Bach on the radio. One night in Denver four of us arranged to meet at a triple-A restaurant. Sally showed up in a red velvet evening gown, white fur stole and tiara. She had ordered our wines in advance by telephone.

Above and beyond all this, Sally was an extraordinary cook. On the road in Texas, for somebody's birthday she baked a *genoise* cake in her motel room; the white icing with perfect little rosettes looked so beautiful nobody wanted to cut into it. Back in New York, she gave a dinner party in her apartment for the entire company, stagehands, producers, creators, et al.—thirty to forty people. While the composer Jule Styne sat at Sally's spinet playing out-take numbers from the show, some of which seemed to be about how underneath it all Rose was a nice person, a few of us blew kisses to the memory of Jerome Robbins for cutting them. Sally sat calmly on a stool just inside her kitchen in a blue velvet dress with a ribbon in her hair, stirring chocolate for the hand-dipped candies she later served for dessert while we jostled each other to get to the main course, Chicken Kiev. Chicken Kiev for forty. Think about it.

Sally—funny, generous, unfathomable. I hope wherever she is, she's getting the love she deserves.

Going On

BESIDES PLAYING TESSIE, I WAS ALSO UNDERSTUDYING ANGELA Lansbury's Rose. I loved working on the part, and having regular rehearsals on the road gave structure to my days, but it didn't occur to me that I would ever have to go on for Angela. Angela was a strong, energetic woman. I felt perfectly safe. When we got to Los Angeles, however, I was told that I would be going on as Rose in a special matinee performance.

Nothing before or since has ever frightened me as much as this. I was told three weeks in advance, which gave me plenty of time to turn to stone. I rehearsed daily with the understudies, but in the shower I could not recall the lyrics beyond "Some people can—," the opening number.

The show had an electronic runway that moved out over the orchestra pit for "Rose's Turn," and one day Baby June's British stage mother saw me practicing on it backstage. "You want to be very careful, you know," she offered, "you could so easily fall into the pit and hurt yourself." Life imitating art. Angela told me to just keep my eyes on the runway lights and I would be fine. She showed me where in "Rose's Turn" it was possible to grab a couple of deep breaths. "Remember to breathe," she said. This is possibly the best advice I ever got about performing in general.

On the day before D-Day, I did a run-through with the actual cast. We performed in an airless rehearsal room for the producers and staff. They were sitting inches away from me, along the wall, and I shouted into their stony faces, number after number. Nobody rushed to me afterwards to assure me of a job well done.

The theater was the immense Los Angeles Schubert, with its two thousand one hundred semi-reclined, plush velvet seats, no center aisle. As the overture started, unseen hands guided me through steel doors and down endless concrete hallways to the back of the house, to the aisle I would come down, clutching my miniature Yorkie and shouting, "Sing out, Louise!" The next thing I knew, I was standing onstage in total darkness, I couldn't think, hear, or see. As the intro to my first song started, I began to make out the conductor's face through the blackness. He had a large white face, like a moon. I watched this moon as it mouthed each lyric just ahead of the beat. I made it through. I made it through the next moment and the next, and the darkness began to recede, bit by bit.

I didn't have to think about which scene came next as unseen hands guided me to each new entrance. Then, suddenly, before "Rose's Turn," there was nobody there. I was standing alone in the dark, flipping the velour curtains muttering, "Where, where?" when there below me I saw the little runway lights; the runway was moving out over the orchestra pit. It seemed like a couple of miles to the other end. With her long legs, Angela had sprinted across it like a gazelle. I was the size of a peanut next to her. Somehow I made it—I got through it all without collapse. I had a large supply of very real desperation for Rose's last "For me! For me!" There were many actors in the audience that day who could appreciate the understudy's ordeal. They gave me a wonderful reception.

After the show, a bunch of us drove to Joe Allen's bar to celebrate. As we entered, everybody at the bar was turned toward the door and they burst into wild applause. We were amazed to witness this kind of reception in L.A. Once we got inside, we saw the television set above the entrance displaying a football game. They were applauding a touchdown.

The British love to tour. Having understudied Angela Lansbury in *Gypsy*, Jane Connell said, "Oh, Mary Louise, you are going to clean up in summer stock!" meaning I would get to play Rose in places like the Melody Fair tent in North Tonawanda, New York. Now the truth is, I have no desire to play the provinces, and I loathe tents. But I needn't have worried, because after a successful run in the West End, then touring the U.S. for six months, and then playing ten months on Broadway, Angela went on for the entire summer circuit, including North Tonawanda, New York.

On the Road

I'VE BEEN ON THE ROAD THREE TIMES. ONE GENERAL RULE IS, THE farther away the cast gets from home the more they start sleeping around. You fall into bed with people you wouldn't ordinarily throw sticks at. At the same time, you become extremely finicky about whom you eat with. Everybody knew who was sleeping with whom and didn't care, but there were clandestine meetings about where to eat. "*Psst*, meet us on the corner. We're going to O'Reilly's, but don't tell Don!" Listening to the sweet little character man describe his preference for the *haricot vert* over the green bean for the fortieth time acted on me like a hot cattle prod up my ass. He had to go. Likewise the character actress who was in the habit of pummeling the waiter with instructions, her lamb rare but not bloody, her salad with the tomatoes, cucumber, lettuce, and dressing on the side, the nuts removed from the nut roll.

You had to be extremely careful. As you headed out, you would hear behind you plaintive bleats; "Where's everybody going?" "Where are you all going to eat?" and if you didn't immediately scoot around a corner, you would find yourself entering a restaurant in a mournful herd. Table for forty, please. It would take an hour to get a waiter, another to give the orders, another for the food to arrive, and a final two for the Division of the Dinner Check. This was a mathematical nightmare usually cheerfully undertaken by the actor who had a degree in accounting and who wanted to know who had the whipped cream on his pecan pie because that was ten cents extra. In the end, the pot usually came up short because when it was time to pay up somebody was usually in the john.

In *Gypsy*, Denny and Sally and I liked to dine together in fancy restaurants. For starters, Sally would order a baked Alaska with chocolate ice cream and a stinger, and when the waiter's eyebrows shot up she sweetly exclaimed, "People don't realize how good mint and chocolate are together!" No squabbling over the check, we just split it three ways.

Another tour buddy was Rex Robbins, who played Herbie. We had worked together in Julius Monk revues. On previous tours Rex had befriended local citizens in every town, and they would invite him to dine with them. I was appalled by the idea of spending time with the locals, but in Oklahoma City he persuaded me to come along with a couple who took us to dinner in a revolving restaurant on top of the tallest building in town, which was maybe ten floors high. As the restaurant turned, we viewed a gas tank, an empty field, and a couple of cows.

In L.A., Rex persuaded me to go with him on our dinner break between shows to a pool party given by a woman we knew from our Julius Monk days. He said there would be plenty of food. As we drove up, the woman gestured to us from behind a tall fence to come through the gate. This was the seventies, remember: we entered just as a nude guy rose from his lawn chair and strolled to the bar with a leaf stuck to his bottom. All the guests were nude, including our hostess, who had a horrifying scar across her belly. I struggled not to stare—it was like trying not to notice a boa constrictor. Everybody was not looking anywhere, faking nonchalance. Rex sportingly wore a small towel, I clung to my bikini. But what infuriated me most was that there was nothing to eat besides salsa and chips.

WHEN GIVEN A CHOICE OF DRESSING ROOMS, I OPT FOR EITHER A private or a ward. During the New York run of *Gypsy* at the Winter Garden Theater, Sally, Denny, the new Mazeppa Gloria Rossi, and I asked to share a dressing room, which was ideal. We could be silent when we chose or gab our heads off. We had a wonderful time together. No semiprivates; I was once trapped in a dressing room in a long run of *How to Succeed in Business* with one other person and her telephone, and her endless conversations combined with the piped-in music of Burt Bacharach was my idea of hell on earth. A ward is the best; the play always goes better when all the actors are in the same room. All in the same room and all paid the same. Things go wonderfully well onstage.

The de Lys dressing room was a narrow galley divided into stalls. It was up a steep flight of stairs and you had to squeeze past the enormous, grim-faced wardrobe woman sitting like Cerberus at the top. She scared the hell out of me. The pay phone was on the wall over her head; actors just leaned into her immovable bulk to make calls. Opening night telegrams were sent to former cast members who had moved on; every time the same message: "A warm hand on your opening." Foul language, raspberries, and fart noises flew between the stalls; I felt like Bo Peep in their midst. It was a breeding ground for the raunch required onstage.

Performing *Royal Family* in Washington, the Kennedy Center dressing rooms were chilly, bathroom-tiled cells a few floors below the theater. You took an elevator. The elevator was as big as a living room, I suppose for deploying scenery as well as actors; it moved at the speed of a snail. I was filled with angst; I couldn't imagine how to gauge the time I would need to make my cue. When it finally let me off, I was in the middle of a vast space, empty except for a basketball court; in the distance I could make out the tiny box of the stage area itself. I ended up hanging around in the wings when offstage.

On the television show *One Day at a Time*, my dressing room was a brown cubicle with a sofa, table, and lamp. Air occasionally blew in through a vent in the wall. In the expectation of making the place more personal, I left my toothbrush and a book behind, but it turned out the rooms were used by actors on other shows on other days. I spent centuries in that hole during tech rehearsals, lying on the hard sofa, smoking jays, in an existential drift.

The hallway leading from my dressing room to the set was lined with doors opening onto offices with people busily shoving things into printers and typing away, not even glancing up as I wobbled past in my stiletto heels and tootsie getup. What these offices were doing there I have no idea. I could have passed by wearing nothing but the stilettos and they still wouldn't have looked up.

The idea is that you learn from exaggeration.

—D.V.

The Mink

WHEN THE *GYPSY* TOUR BEGAN TO HEAD BACK TOWARD BROAD-way, I started to obsess about what I would wear to the opening night party at Sardi's. I was forty-one, I had a great role in a hit show, and I was flush with money, so I decided that what I needed was a mink coat. Stuck in my mind was the image of Bette Davis in *All About Eve*, half into her mink and wearing one diamond earring. The quintessential Broadway actress. What was she wearing underneath? I don't know, who cares? So in Chicago, Philly, D.C., and Boston, I visited fur salons with Sally—Sally, of course, knew a great deal about furs. She knew about pelts. We sat on a sofa while the salesman slapped furs down on the carpet and wiggled them backwards so we could examine the pelts. We must have looked at a hundred minks. I couldn't find the classic Bette Davis style. Finally, in that desperate sweat when you are about to spend an obscene amount of money on something you know in your heart isn't the One, I chose a princess-style mink with sable cuffs and collar. Beautiful, but not really me.

Opening night came, I put on my mink and sailed into Sardi's. The hat-check girl tried to take it from me. I demurred, went to my table. After fifteen minutes I was suffocating. I realized that I wouldn't be able to eat without dipping a sable cuff into the marinara sauce, so I had to take it off. Underneath I was wearing a boring little black jersey dress.

This is when I learned a valuable rule: Before you buy an expensive item, remember that it's going to require maintenance. Manhattan was crime-ridden in the seventies. I was afraid my apartment might get robbed so I got one of the *Gypsy* carpenters to build a secret panel into my closet to hide the mink. The only problem was that there was a hot water pipe in the wall, and it was pointed out to me that heat was death to mink. This was around the time I was getting calls every other week to fly to L.A. for television tests. I took the mink with me in a pillowcase. It was easy because, really, you cannot imagine how lightweight real fur is.

And really, until you have slept under it in sub-zero weather, you have no idea how warm real fur can be.

The *Gypsy* tour ended just before Christmas. Denny and I set out to spend the holiday at my house upstate. We started off in unusually mild weather, but as we drove north the temperature began to plummet. There was no heat in my little VW Beetle. Snow was falling in buckets. We had to stop talking because our breath was fogging up the windshield. Finally we reached the house, slogged through ten-foot drifts to the front door, stepped inside, and were greeted by the sound of gushing water and a freezing interior. The furnace was off and pipes had burst. Nothing cut the cold out until we were huddled nose to nose under the mink. That silly mink saved our lives. Eventually, having no place to wear it, I sold it to the Ritz Thrift Shop on West 57th Street.

M ARK AND I WERE FINDING MORE AND MORE ARTICLES ABOUT Vreeland with quotes from people who knew her:

At the center of this outrageous whirlwind lay a rigorous, controlling eye.

One look at her pen-stroke physique, her strictly ordered desk, her regimented routines, or her reductive office uniform of dark separates betrayed the sober face behind the party mask.

She was not wild: she was a disciplined savage . . . she worked fantastically hard. She brought seduction to the workplace. She combined seduction with encouragement. Manners and behavior were paramount . . . She was the ultimate in refinement.

She was the most unsnobby person I've ever known. Like most grand people, she was mentally humble.

She was great because she was inquisitive. She enthused people because of her inquisitiveness.

She was always on time. And she never failed to thank people for the smallest thing. Of course, she was very theatrical and very exceptional . . . she was one of the most tolerant people I have ever known. She never criticized, she had humor, she had great courage, she had understanding, kindness, and she had depth.

WE NEEDED TO COMPOSE CONNECTIVE TISSUE BETWEEN THE stories. We needed to re-create Vreeland's idiosyncratic speech. I thought of the famous monologist Ruth Draper. I actually saw her perform at a matinee on Broadway soon after I arrived in the city. I was completely entranced. I couldn't believe it when I heard on the radio three days later that she had died. It was a tremendous thing that somebody thought to make recordings of her monologues. The list of people who love her is long and disparate: Mike Nichols, Lily Tomlin, Charles Busch, Julie Harris, Tom Waits, John Gielgud and Uta Hagen were just a few of her fans.

I knew by heart Draper's sublime monologue, "The Italian Lesson." The society matron's conversation is littered with references to jade eggs, brass frogs, yellow lamp shades, golf clubs, pigeon pie, camembert cheese, Dante, Virgil, and puppies. Vreeland, who had the bottoms of her shoes polished and her money ironed, was similarly pre-occupied with detail.

I liked also the Orson Welles school of action, beginning in mid-stream, so I wanted, as the lights came up on the empty living room, to hear Vreeland's voice offstage giving orders:

Ice! Plenty of ice! And Scotch! If there is any, Mr. Adlerberg likes Scotch. STOP! Pull all those old serviettes out of there and throw them away. Don't tell me "no"! Only beautiful things! If you can't do that, clear out! Now, the florist is send-ing over peonies, parrot tulips, Madonna lilies, and the whole bit? He also promised me some very large branches of forced quince. And then she enters talking: *I want this room in FLAMES!*"

1993: *Full Gallop* Juilliard Benefit

*A*S THE RESULT OF A CASUAL REFERENCE TO OUR PLAY ON A BUS from upstate to Manhattan, we managed to get a one-night gig at a benefit in the city. Margot Harley, head of the Acting Company, was sitting next to Mark Chmiel, an actor friend of mine. She happened to mention she was looking for something to present and Mark, bless him, mentioned my play and she remembered seeing the reading at the Cosmopolitan Club.

*B*EFORE THIS READING, I SCREWED MY NERVE TO THE STICKING place and telephoned Paul Huntley, the undisputed king of wig design. Before Paul had arrived from England, wigs were made out of horse hair, and everybody who wore them looked like Princess Tonawanda, even the men. Actors tended not to wear wigs at all unless they were playing Hawaiians. After Paul arrived on the scene, productions of all sizes, types, and periods started using wigs. His creations were transforming. As Miss Prism in a production of *The Importance of Being Earnest*, he gave me pale, thinning wisps. I appeared to be slightly balding. As First Witch, he gave me a long, tangled mane. So I called him: might he have an old hank of hair lying around somewhere that I could use to play Vreeland for this performance?

"Well, darling," he said in his lovely British accent, "Is this for charity?" I said it was, and he said, "Well then, why don't I just make you a wig?"

He not only made it, he came to the performance to put it on me. That wig was utterly transforming. In his hands it looked like a little marmoset; on my head, I was Vreeland. It strengthened my faltering belief that this play was really going to happen.

I wore this wig through all the proceeding productions. After the yearlong run off Broadway, when I left to reprise it in England, Paul refurbished it and stuck a beautiful little tortoise-shell comb in the little hump at the top.

*I*WAS PERFORMING ON A SET FOR ANOTHER PLAY, BUT WE MANAGED to get a proper sofa arranged on it. At this point we hadn't staged it, I was still just sitting there, talking.

We needed to hire a maid. We asked a friend of a friend of Mark's. I've forgotten her name. My only memory of her was her complaint later that she caught a bad cold that night, and for weeks afterwards we heard how it developed into the flu and then pneumonia, and from there to a long hospital stay. I knew it would be hard to find anybody aside from a complete nut to play this role.

The house was packed and they roared. Afterwards people surrounded me. It was a thrilling night. I thought we were surely launched. A producer I knew, Edgar Rosenblum, was there, and I fished, "Well, what did you think?" He smiled enigmatically and said, "Ditch the maid."

*A*FTER THE JUILLIARD READING, MARK AND I WERE RUNNING UP all avenues, looking under rocks for anybody who might have the slightest connection with Mrs. Vreeland or fashion, and could help us get produced. The fashion people we approached either refused to speak to us or were extremely amenable, like Boaz Mazor who worked for Oscar de la Renta. Boaz Mazor is, as quoted by others, "One of the nicest men in New York Society, one of the nicest in International Society, one of the nicest in the world." And he was lovely to us. We made friends with D.D. Ryan, a socialite who worshiped Vreeland. We never knew what Vreeland thought of D.D. She affected a Japanese-mask look: chalk white makeup, hair dyed black-black, parted in the middle and pulled tight on her skull into braids. Lips scarlet, of course. I remembered seeing her in the audience at Julius Monk's shows. She had seen us at Bay Street and was very moved. She showed me the right shoes to wear for Vreeland. Mark and I met her for lunch at Shun Lee a few times. But there was no future for our play there. Generally, fashion people have a deaf eye for theater. They deal in surfaces. The ones who were interested could only conceive of our play as a commercial for a fashion show. We were always looking for backers, but I realize now, fashion people are always looking for backers for themselves.

She had a very special manner of placing her feet when she walked through the corridors of Vogue. Her studied equilibrium was such, one imagined her walking through a palace.

THE ONE THING WE COULDN'T FIND WAS ANY FILM OF DIANA walking. She walked like a ballet dancer, on the balls of her feet, hips thrust forward. Decades of models walked down the runway like her. Diana glided. They glided. By pure chance I mentioned to Carmine Porcelli, a fashion designer I knew, that I was working on a play about her. He not only knew her but had dined several times in her famous living room and this guy wasn't an actor, but he perfectly imitated her mannerisms, particularly her walk. He glided beautifully.

Even so, I wanted to find film showing her walking so I could study it. Mark heard about a video the late Andy Warhol had made of her. Various people were in charge of his estate, there was some sort of museum in the works, and we got a number to call. Those times when we had to try to breach the walls of one or another snooty defender of the Vreeland cult in order to get something, information or papers we needed, I felt like an Oakie. Not dressed well enough. I didn't have the right shoes.

The Warholians were vague and withholding on the telephone; the harder it got the more it became something I simply had to have, the most valuable bit of information we could possibly acquire. After several calls, we were finally informed we might pick up a copy of the video at the desk. The receptionist stared at us, we sidled in bowing and scraping and grabbed it.

Having scored a coup, we took ourselves to the Edison Hotel coffee shop for a celebratory breakfast. The Edison is a traditional hangout for old character actors. It was around the corner from *Prelude to a Kiss*, which I was in at the time and I had a matinee that day. I ordered eggs Benedict and scarfed them down. Minutes later my stomach seized up. I doubled over in an agonizing cramp. I thought I was going to pass out, so I lay down on the booth seat. I couldn't see or hear what Mark was doing, he seemed to be sitting there like a wooden statue. I felt I was going to erupt. I asked the waitress passing by where the bathroom was, she said I had to go across the hotel lobby. I staggered from the booth to the door leading into the lobby. It was crammed with German tourists in lederhosen. I didn't think I could make it and crawled back. Couldn't I use the john in the restaurant? Our waitress must have seen this sort of thing often, she was completely blasé. She said this john is for the help only. By this time I was groaning like a wounded buffalo. Management called an ambulance. I was lifted onto a stretcher, and as I was carried out past the customers, I heard a guy sitting in the aisle remark to his buddy, "That's the gal who was on *One Day at a Time*."

The minute I got into the ambulance the pain stopped. We hadn't even left the curb. The ambulance guy looked at me suspiciously, "You okay now?" I mumbled an apology and climbed out. I made it to the theater in time for the half-hour call.

The tape turned out to show Vreeland thoroughly ensconced on her couch, listening to the endless dronings of an art curator named Henry Geldzahler.

Every time the project took a step forward, I seemed to develop some physical ailment. When we first got permission to write the play, I developed a back pain so bad I couldn't sit upright for two weeks. Then I developed a throbbing toothache during the Playwrights' reading, and now after getting the Warhol tape I nearly exploded at the Edison. What was up with that? I had no idea.

Ellis Rabb

I MET ELLIS RABB THROUGH NICKY MARTIN. ELLIS WAS TALL, WILLOWY, silly, kind, selfish, extremely theatrical, and terribly funny. He was an instinctive director and a genius at casting. He directed and acted in highly successful revivals of classic plays on Broadway with A.P.A., his company of actors I would have given my left kidney to work with.

I almost got to work with him when, in 1973, he was set to direct a Broadway revival of *The Women*, starring Alexis Smith, Kim Hunter, and Myrna Loy. He didn't audition actors. He had seen me in *Gypsy*. He called me up and in a low, melodious voice asked, "Which would you rather play, darling? Nancy the writer? Or the maid?" I could hardly believe my ears. Of course I told him I preferred the writer. He said, "Do you darling? Then it's yours." However, when the producers insisted on hiring the movie actress Rhonda Fleming for the Paulette Goddard role, Ellis quit the production. We were passed on to Morton "Teke" DaCosta, who had apparently recovered from *Hot Spot* and happily crocheted a large afghan while rehearsing us. During the first act, each time a star made an entrance, he directed me to cross the stage and light a cigarette, until the fourth time when I pointed out that I was now holding three lit cigarettes in my hand.

Doris Dowling

O N THE FIRST DAY OF REHEARSALS FOR *THE WOMEN*, AMIDST THE pretty young things, old character actresses, faded stage names, and one or two film legends milling around the ballroom, I spied a vision in leopard fur and veiled derby, nervously twiddling a gold lorgnette. She looked like a forties B-movie actress. She *was* a forties B-movie actress: Doris Dowling. She played Alan Ladd's wife in *The Blue Dahlia* and the girl in the bar in *The Lost Weekend*. She was darkly beautiful: raven brows, thick eyelashes, delicate bone structure. As a teenager she danced with the Ballet Russe de Monte Carlo. She was a young beauty in *Bitter Rice*, the first postwar Italian film to come to the U.S. She was the seventh of bandleader Artie Shaw's eight wives. In Hollywood, Doris was a girlfriend of Billy Wilder. I quite liked her. A few of us shared a dressing room. Without a shred of irony, she cautioned us that when flowers were delivered backstage we must be careful not to throw the box away before searching for the jewelry.

Doris had tons of real jewelry. And furs, lots of furs. She was an interesting mixture of street tough and cultivated lady. Her European youth no doubt accounted for her exquisite table manners. It was a pleasure to dine out with her. She ate her meal leisurely, pleasurably. She was imperious but never rude to the waiters, making them want to die for her. Over the next few years, her Beverly Hills bungalow became an oasis for me whenever I had to spend time in the L.A. desert. She liked to cook delicacies like braised endive and blancmange. On the other hand her taste in paintings leaned toward large oils by seventies' Los Angeles artists depicting nudes writhing in space with smoke shooting out of their nipples.

Doris rolled her joints in leopard-print papers from the famous lingerie store, Frederick's of Hollywood. One time we got in her souped-up former stuntman's Chevy—"Engine by Fisher," she informed me—and shared a joint as we roared downtown to hear a bicentennial concert by John Cage. It was unforgettable. Music stands and huge speakers littered the stage. A Native American in sunglasses stood at a mike stage right. Stage left at a mike was a small woman in black with tightly coiled white hair. Every now and then during the cacophony, the Native American would start to laugh. A low, mocking laugh. At other moments, the little woman stage left would start singing, "Oh, the lamb of God . . ." Half the audience left. We loved it.

1976: *The Royal Family*

*E*LLIS RABB OFFERED ME THE PART OF KITTY LEMOYNE IN *THE Royal Family*. I didn't want to do it, the part was so small. There were rumors that Ellis wasn't going to pull it off, and as weeks passed without further word, I wondered if it would happen at all. Meanwhile I heard about this other play, *A Matter of Gravity* by Enid Bagnold, and starring Katharine Hepburn. I loved Bagnold's plays, and I'd worshiped Hepburn ever since the night I saw her on Dick Cavett's show, when he asked her why she had no children and she fairly bellowed, "YOU CAN'T HAVE IT ALL!"

The part I wanted to play was Hepburn's maid. She was described as an alcoholic lesbian who levitated when she was upset. I had to have this part. I marched into the casting woman's office, a kindly lady who looked worried. "But aren't you doing *Royal Family*?" I asked her to let me read anyway. The maid was supposed to be fat. I wrapped towels around my middle under a loose dress. This was one of the very few times I went after a role. I was asked to come back and read again for Ms. Hepburn. Strangely, that night I was watching a low-budget British vampire film on TV and recognized the director of *Gravity* playing the vampire. He was very hammy. I read again, but then I was given the date for first rehearsal of *Royal Family*, so that was that.

I played Kitty LeMoyne, a Cavendish in name only. Here is the authors' description of her: *About forty, but doesn't believe it. An actress for many years, never more than mediocre.* This description infuriated me. Even the authors detested her. I crossed it out. Of course I, Kitty, believed I was just as good an actress as any of these Cavendishes.

Seventy-eight-year-old Eva Le Gallienne played the family matriarch, Rosemary Harris played her actress daughter. The John Barrymore role was George Grizzard and, later, Ellis himself. Fanny's brother and my husband was Joe Maher, and the role of the manager was Sam Levene. Grand actors each and every one.

This play was to be part of a series of American plays produced by Roger Stevens, then head of the Kennedy Center in Washington, D.C. It was given to Ellis to direct and on the first day of rehearsals he told us he didn't know what it was about. I felt the same when I read it, it seemed to be nothing more than a series of entrances and exits and breakfasts and telephone calls and shouting matches. We had been rehearsing for about a week when Ellis suddenly stood up and in his drawling baritone said, "I have just realized what this play is about. Everybody gets *work!*" This was a terrific insight. This play was about actors entering, exiting, having breakfast, making phone calls, and having shouting matches. Actors marry, have children, get sick, go blind and die, but above all that, there's the work. If an actor is a pallbearer at his mother's funeral and he gets a call, he'll drop the coffin and hop in a taxi.

Sam Levene kept his hat on all through rehearsals. He skulked in corners studying his script, and if I said good morning to him he gave a surly grunt and turned away. One morning I came into the rehearsal room early when only he and the stage manager were there. Suddenly emboldened, I said, "Mr. Levene, I dreamt about you last night." This was true, I had. "I dreamt you took me to Paris. You invited me to a drug store and bought me a seltzer." He grunted "Yeah?" I didn't realize that I had made a friend.

The day before our first tryout in Princeton, Sam came over to me and asked if I was driving down and could he get a lift. I gulped. There he was the next day, this famous and famously grumpy movie actor standing on my doorstep with his Gladstone bag. We drove down the New Jersey Turnpike in my VW Beetle in the pouring rain. That night he took me to dinner and told me his life story. It was the saddest story I'd ever heard. He only married once, late in life, to a "beautiful young girl" and she gave him a son, but he left her. Why? He shrugged. He didn't know why. He loved her but he had to leave her. He moved into a room at the Hotel St. Moritz, where he lived for the rest of his life.

There was a point in the play when Joe, Le Gallienne and I waited offstage in the so-called library, while onstage Levene delivered a long, eloquent speech to Rosemary. Joe and I paced back and forth, smoking (incredible now to think we were allowed to smoke backstage!), while LeG sat in a chair. One night she crooked a finger at me; I came over, and as Sam's speech went on, she hissed, "This should be cut." The play was three hours long, but Ellis fluted, "I can't possibly cut any of it, because it's all *texture*." Another time LeG called me over and whispered, "I was horrid tonight. I was like Helen *Haaaayes*," dragging out the word in a mordant tone. I demurred heartily in pantomime and walked away. She called me back and whispered; "She's not a friend of yours, is she?"

The theater we were in was called the Helen Hayes. Le Gallienne had starred in *The Swan* in this same theater in the thirties when it was called the Fulton. Joe and I always called it the Fulton in her presence.

This was an old-fashioned play with a large cast and several people sitting onstage at one time. I was on the whole first act and had very few lines. I worried how I was going to keep from losing focus, sitting there all that time with no lines. I remembered this actress I knew who, when you bumped into her, her eyes roamed all over your person while talking to you until she would suddenly interrupt the conversation to demand to know where you got your shoes or your dress or who cut your hair. She molested friends with her eyes, desiring this girl's suit and that girl's scarf. "Is that a Liberty blouse?!" "Where did you get that necklace?!" "Are those real leather?!" and so on. This mentality was wonderfully useful to me. As I watched Rosemary Harris float down the stairs in lavender chiffon each night, I would think, "I saw that same dress in pink in *Vogue* magazine," or, "Lavender doesn't suit her at all." Or I would look at Joe and note that he had put on some pounds, or look at Sam to see if he was going bald. It served me well night after night.

After Princeton, we went to the Kennedy Center in D.C. *A Matter of Gravity* was also in town. I ran into Christopher Reeve, who was in it, and he went into a heartbreaking spiel about the miserable experience he was having. Hepburn wouldn't let anybody move, not even their faces, and Ms. Bagnold kept running down the aisle in a tea gown and bare feet, yelling at the actors. Chris said she had wooden teeth. So much for idols.

In Washington the audience thought I was a bitch. They greeted my lines with little gasps, or *"tsk tsk"* noises, as if I was delivering gross insults. Kitty made tactless remarks, was stupid and silly and wore vulgar hats, but I didn't think she deserved to be hated. That's when I realized the role had been written as a foil for the noble Cavendishes. I was there to make them look superior.

New York audiences found Kitty funny, a great relief to me, but double-edged; in New York, Kitty was a pariah. The terrible thing was I couldn't separate myself from the role. When people told me how good they thought I was, it made me miserable. No matter how I sliced it, it was painful. I spent hours weeping inconsolably in the therapist's office.

Actors, if they're any good, tend to take on the personalities of the characters they're playing. While I was suffering more and more, the members of the Cavendish family were becoming more and more grandiose. After a while it seemed they were starting to overreact to me. I happened to glance upstage once, on my first entrance, and saw the actress who played the maid going berserk with grimaces and gestures of distaste. I hadn't even said anything yet. In the second act, night after night, just as I began to speak to LeG, as if I was vapor Rosemary leaned over to her and started whispering in her ear, apparently about the toilet running in the upstairs loge. (The theater was on its last legs; it rained onstage.) Then I began noticing Joe Maher rolling his eyes just as I started to speak. I loved Joe; we were drinking buddies. Now, though, I was wishing he wouldn't do what he was doing. I decided to speak to him; I went to his dressing room. "Joe, could I ask you to not roll your eyes until after I've finished my line?" A brief silence, followed by an explosion. His face turned the color of maroon pajamas and his eyes bulged dangerously: "How DARE you accuse me of doing such a thing? How DARE you criticize my acting?" I was aghast. He scared the hell out of me.

Still, I wasn't imagining it, I was being preempted. Nobody believes this kind of thing happens, but it does. It does. If you play a despicable character, you should prepare to be treated despicably, and not excluding stage management and the general public.

In fact, the general public is great at this game. At those cocktail parties where the patrons get to mingle with the actors, players of kings are treated like royalty, commoners are ignored, and anybody playing a servant, if standing too near, is apt to be handed a napkin full of olive pits.

Anyway, years after the fact I was telling my friend, actress Carol Morley, how hurt my feelings were in *Royal Family*, and Carol shot back, "That's why you were so good!" God bless her.

I DON'T CARE IF IT'S ELEONORA DUSE UP THERE, ACTORS WILL KILL to get their laughs. Actors everywhere are cherishing their laughs. King Lear is looking out for his laughs: "Hey, you know when I turn to Regan and tell her to butt out? I get a nice little laugh there." And Gloucester thinks, That's my laugh! When I give him that look!

They'll also try to kill, at least maim, any laughs you're getting. Lynn Redgrave told this story about being in her first play, in a scene with Dame Edith Evans. First night out, Lynn, seated in a chair, got a nice little laugh on her line. The next night, just as she finished the line, Dame Edith crossed in back of the chair to the other side of the stage and killed it. So Lynn knocked timidly on Dame Edith's dressing room door; "Oh, Dame Edith, I have this nice little laugh there where I'm sitting on the chair, and I wonder if I could trouble you to just wait for it before you start your cross." And Dame Edith replied, "Of course, darling! I'm so sorry I didn't notice!" The next night, Lynn said the line and Dame Edith again immediately made her cross. Lynn said, "Dame Edith, could you possibly hold your cross until I've said the line?" Dame Edith: "Certainly, dear girl, certainly." The next night, the same thing happened again. Finally, the night after that, Lynn said her line, then stuck her foot out and blocked Dame Edith's cross, at which point Dame Edith whispered, "You're learning, darling, you're learning."

In the all-star production of *The Women*, when Rhonda Fleming joined the cast, she co-opted most of my character's lines ("I'm Mary's best friend, shouldn't I be saying that?"), but I still had enough wise-cracks left. Nobody paid much attention until we were in front of an audience and I got laughs. One by one, the stars called me into their dressing rooms. Sitting on a silk chaise with Alexis Smith: "You got a laugh on that line," she said, as if I had swallowed a goldfish in the middle of things. "Yes" I replied. "I must leave a space for it," she said. "Please don't," I said, but it was no use.

In the sixties I played the ingénue in *The Milliken Breakfast Show*, starring the Cowardly Lion, Bert Lahr. We had a tiny scene together, maybe four lines, and I got a couple of laughs. After the first show I was summoned to his dressing room. He squinted at me and said, "Whaddever you're doing, cuddidout."

Funny men can't abide funny women; they go berserk. When you get a laugh, they look at you like you just stuck a shiv in their gut. In *The Philadelphia Story*, at Lincoln Center, in a scene with this one actor, he managed to preempt the laughs I was getting by emitting strategically timed "whoops." Just at the end of each line I spoke, he let out a "whoop." I couldn't believe his gall. The theater was so huge you could imagine that nobody out there heard him, but I heard him, and to this day I'd like to strangle him.

In *The Gnädiges Fräulein* in Baltimore, the Cockaloonie Bird was played by a resident mime; all during my monologue he was jumping and leaping and pooping and running around upstage of me. When I asked him to cool it, he said, "I can't help it. I'm a bird!"

If you can't get laughs, there's always weeping. I played Martha in *Who's Afraid of Virginia Woolf?* in Rochester, New York, and the actor playing George started weeping as soon as we came in the door from the party, and continued to weep for the rest of the evening. One night I heard an audience member mutter about me, "Boy, what a ball-buster!"

May 1993: Woodstock

Woodstock, New York, is about a half hour away from my home upstate. One day Gloria, a dour, humorless woman I knew only slightly, approached me. She had overheard me talking about my play and said she was forming a woman's theater company in Woodstock and suggested she produce it. And so we put it on in the art gallery there for three weekends in May.

After much agony Mark and I had finally settled on the stories we could use. There wasn't any place for the one about being poolside in Sidi Bou Said and spotting King Farouk lounging on what appeared to be big pink pillows, until he got up and she realized the pillows were him; or the one about how a formula for chip-free nail enamel that she, Vreeland, brought over from her Parisian manicurist ended up in the hands of a young Charles Revson. It was agony to jettison these and other stories we loved, but they had to be at least somewhat relevant to the moment.

This time, Mark got his mate Michael Sharp to design the set. Michael was a real artist, and he created a beautiful set that we later discovered would have to be dismantled every night after the show so that the gallery could function as usual during the day. What with the "management" which consisted of Gloria and her "producer" sidekick Jerry, a hyperactive hairdresser who commuted from Poughkeepsie and when needed was never anywhere to be found, the dismantling usually fell on Mark to do. The "management" was heavily into EST and they were often stuck in a weepy hug in the middle of the aisle when we were trying to set up.

An actress Mark knew, Kate Skinner, volunteered to play the maid. She was too young and pretty for the role, but she was still game. We had a lot of fun together. It was early May and the quince bushes were in bloom, and on the drive to Woodstock Mark and I kept spotting quince bushes in front yards and stopping to steal branches for Vreeland's floral arrangement.

I made my entrance through the EXIT door. If it was raining outside, I entered with an umbrella. To get the audience in the proper mood, we played Louis Armstrong singing "You Do Something to Me" as they settled into their seats. We wanted them to feel they were at a cocktail party. However, just when things were pleasantly abuzz, the music was cut off and Gloria stumped out. In a voice of doom she thanked people for coming, asked for money, and then droned on about the next play about breast cancer. As she stumped off the lights went up, and on with the show! Gloria's speech got longer and more doleful with every performance. We stood backstage listening to it metastasize.

Jerry, who ran the lights and the phone buzzers, didn't show up one day, and Mark, hysterical, had to do it all. This whole thing reeked of flop sweat. However, we had full houses the entire run, predominately women. It hadn't occurred to me before that the play had a special appeal as the story of an older woman overcoming the odds. One of the great things about Vreeland was that she had a successful life.

Was it a happy one? I don't know, but it was the life she chose, and she didn't end up on a slag heap.

June 1993: Bay Street

A FEW WEEKS AFTER WOODSTOCK, WE GOT A NIBBLE FROM SYBIL, Sybil Christopher, at the Bay Street Theater in Sag Harbor. We were invited to perform five readings, but we were past readings now.

Once again, Michael Sharp did the set, and this time there was much more to it. Mark had these huge screens made and brought out from Manhattan in a rented van. The sofa was rented and covered in red flowered chintz like the one in her Garden in Hell. I didn't question, didn't even think about who paid for it all until months later, when Michael gave me the bill. It was a rude shock; and all mine to pay.

From time to time during rehearsals, I could hear Sybil's deep-throated laughter. I was buoyed by it, but it was hard for me to understand why she kept saying the play should be done in a cabaret setting. She booked the show for two weekends, which meant we didn't have the advantage of reworking the script. The insinuation that the play was too slight to warrant a regular two-week run rankled me.

Here again, the pre-show music was cut off, and the stage manager clunked out and droned on about upcoming shows.

The Sag Harbor audience was embedded with Hamptons socialites. Somebody would rush back and say, "Chessy Rayner's here!" "Pat Buckley's out front!" These ladies left at intermission. When told there was more to the play, they looked surprised, because of course they had dinner parties to attend.

SYBIL INVITED US BACK FOR THREE PERFORMANCES IN THE FALL. "But," she said, "ditch the maid." This time we complied. Kate Skinner was replaced by an intercom.

Through Kate we met a young director, Daniel Fish, and we asked him to direct our play. He had the same fondness we did for the avant garde. The set became more stylized: stacks of Louis Vuitton luggage and pairs of strappy shoes were perched here and there on the stage.

We were still looking for an ending to the play; some kind of "ta-da!" moment. There was this image Mark kept bringing up. He'd gotten into an elevator one day with a bike messenger in a glistening black Lycra bodysuit with one red stripe across the chest, his helmet shiny black with a touch of red, his skin a beautiful chocolate brown. He wanted to see a creature like that onstage with Mrs. Vreeland, perfectly mirroring her. In the same way we'd fantasized about a scene of her having tea at the Savoy with punk rockers, comfortable with their dyed black hair, tattoos, and safety pins in their noses.

We rented *Sid and Nancy*, a film about the Sex Pistol's Sid Vicious, so we could get a look at punk. The film blew our socks off, it was so good, and it gave us a new ending: Vreeland sits on the floor, searching through a spread of fashion photographs as the lights fade, and the house fills with the coke-addled roar of Gary Oldman as Sid Vicious singing "My Way." We loved it, Daniel, Mark and I. They hated it, Sybil and her gang.

Pilot Season

THERE IS THIS PHENOMENON CALLED "PILOT SEASON," SOMETHING like the salmon run. For a couple of weeks, casting agents put actors on tape for dozens of new television pilots.

Being put on tape means it doesn't matter so much what you wear from the waist down, but eyeglasses are a problem. I'm blind without mine. I try to memorize the lines, but I'm not a quick study, and if I lose them I can't see the script, all of which makes for a stuttering mess. The actor usually reads with the casting assistant, a perky young woman who is standing in for Sean Penn or Johnny Depp. "Read it again, and this time don't act so much," says the young person. I think how easy it would be to be good if you were actually reading with Sean or Johnny. The fact is, I have auditioned on tape eight thousand times over the years, and I have rarely, if ever, been hired as a result.

A big problem for me is the generic role. "Janice, the boss's secretary, smart, wears two-toned shoes, takes no prisoners." "Millie, a good egg, older than she looks, but doesn't like to admit it." I couldn't get a handle on them. It didn't enter my mind when I started out in this business that I would have to impersonate ordinary people.

L.A. in the Seventies

THE ACCEPTED GOAL OF A NEW YORK STAGE ACTOR IS TO LAND A running part on a television series. In the seventies and eighties at least, it meant leaving cold, filthy New York City to live in sunny Los Angeles and make a lot of money. Here's the deal: They put you on tape in New York, the tape went out to the suits in L.A., and if they liked what they saw, they flew you out there for the second audition.

Here's the scenario I went through on a weekly basis for most of the seventies: It's six in the evening, I'm on my second vodka gimlet, and the phone rings; it's the agent, Richard, who just got off the phone with the Coast, where it's only three in the afternoon. The pilot people I went on tape for yesterday want me to fly out at six tomorrow morning for a second audition. While I'm trying to get a grip on this bit of information, he launches into the deal: "A seven-year contract, guaranteed ten out of thirteen episodes, four thousand per episode the first year, going to four-five the second year, five the third, five-five the fourth, six the fifth, and seven the seventh—"

"Waitwaitwait! SEVEN YEARS? I'm only auditioning for Christ's sake!"

"Yes, but if they like you on the Coast, you're hired, so the deal is made now."

"Don't I have to sign something?"

"No. If they want you, it's a done deal."

"But what if the part is no good? Can't I see the script first?"

No. Seven years. Move to the Coast tomorrow for seven years to be on a show on which you don't even know what the part is. But this was what actors dream of. Who cares what the show is? It's L.A.! Beaches! Sunshine! Money!

*E*VEN BEFORE THE PLANE LANDED, MY HAIR DIED. PERFECTLY healthy, bouncy hair lay down flat on my skull. Once on the tarmac, my eyes swelled up. I looked like a prizefighter.

A car would be waiting; I would be driven past oil wells pumping, pumping, pumping, then bungalow, bungalow, bungalow, rugateria, bungalow, bungalow. I was dropped at an office somewhere. I was dying in my woolens. A smiling blonde offered me a bowl of sprouts. Finally I was taken in to read for the suits. Lines like, "Gee, honey, you look pooped!" and "You want some coffee?" I was back on the red-eye to New York that afternoon.

I performed this ritual two or three times a year over a period of ten years. Every now and then I made the grade and filmed a pilot, which, fortunately, was not picked up. The roles I got cast in were generally wives or mothers who said things like, "Mamma mia!" and in the next breath, "So have a little chicken soup, already!" I asked the suits, what was she? Italian or Jewish?" I got blank looks. It eventually dawned on me that they wanted an all-purpose ethnic. Television doesn't deal in specifics. They want to reach the broadest demographic. They're selling soap. That's why soap operas were called that: "Oxydol presents, *Young Doctor Malone!*"

When I bumped into New York actors who had moved out there, they shouted at me, "Isn't this great? No more snow! No more graffiti, no muggers! Look at all this green! I play golf every day! Yatata-TA!" It's true that in the seventies, at least, you could still get somewhere on the freeways, and there were Japanese workers tending lawns with noiseless bamboo rakes and making spectacular arrangements of delicious fruits and vegetables in the giant supermarkets that we didn't yet have on the East Coast. In other words, it was the suburbs. I was terrified of suburbs. I ran from them to the city, to tall dark buildings and crowds and dirt and noise

I could not forgive the blandness of L.A., the boring buildings and rubbery shrubbery, even the birdsong was monotonous. You didn't see people of color on the streets. You didn't see *people*. Nobody walked. You could get arrested. There were hardly any sidewalks anyway. Everyone was in a car behind sunglasses. They could have been naked for all anyone could tell, and yet having just flown in from the East wearing all black, I felt impelled to head immediately to Rodeo Drive and spend a fortune on something in pastel tie-dye.

Once in a while a studio would incarcerate me in a fancy hotel for a few days. There would be a big fruit basket in the room, but the windows were sealed and there was no way to walk outside. I didn't realize how essential to my well-being was the freedom to roam. Daily life in New York was nomadic: I walked everywhere in all kinds of weather, passing all kinds of people, window gazing, stopping for a coffee, shopping for a piece of fish. I needed to escape this prison. I rented a car. But because I was driving I couldn't observe anything, and I didn't have anyplace to drive to.

*I*HAVE ALWAYS HAD A QUARREL WITH SHOW BUSINESS; ALWAYS WANT-ing to run from it, but needing it, needing to be wanted somewhere. My first response to any job offer is invariably "no." I feel like some-body's trying to throw a net over me.

Actors can't afford to offend casting agents by not reading for parts they're suggested for. Only in a dream world would I ever hear my agent say to a casting agent, "Are you kidding? I refuse to let my client read for that! She's way too good for it!" They can't afford to do that any more than I can. But it's always about the role. If it's lousy, I don't want to play it.

When a part is offered outright and I think it's lousy, I can't just say "no thank you." Producers feel they are paying an actor an enor-mous compliment. Their incredulity is understandable. "She's not mar-ried, she has no family, on what possible grounds is she saying no?"

I was always lousy at the business end; I resented having to be interviewed and having to keep up with photos and résumés. I stopped getting new photographs taken of myself after 1989. At least once a year the agent would ask me to send them a hundred new photos, and I wondered what the hell they were doing with them, throwing them out the window? I never seemed to have any on hand myself. When I looked in my file drawer I could never find any and I would think, Who the hell took them? I actually thought somebody must have removed them, it couldn't have been me.

McGraw's

*S*O NOW IT WAS 1993, WE HAD BEEN PLUGGING AWAY FOR THREE years, and making very little progress. We were writing and rewrit-ing, shuffling the running order of stories around. We studied it to find what I kept calling the "MacGuffin." I thought I might be making the word up, but it turned out to be real enough. A MacGuffin is the plot development on which the story turns, or the crucial moment for the protagonist.

In the *Rolling Stone* article, when asked if being fired from *Vogue* upset her, Vreeland said, "Oh yeah, but it didn't last very long. How could it? I mean after all it wasn't a tragedy. It wasn't the end of anything." This was all she said about it publicly, as far as we knew, but we finally realized the play needed a description of the way it happened. Condé Nast was famous for brutal evictions. The description of her last day was the only piece of writing I needed to do that didn't come from her own lips, and it was the toughest.

Then in March of 1994, Murphy Davis, Bay Street Theater's general manager, helped us arrange a backers' audition at McGraw's, a nightclub on West 72nd Street owned by a friend of Mark; we sent out a load of invitations.

This bar had a narrow upstairs room with a tiny stage mostly taken up by a grand piano. We needed something for me to sit on. While Mark and I were struggling to carry a settee up the narrow winding staircase, I completely lost my *joie de vivre*; this was the last straw, lugging my own sofa to perform in a bar. At my age. No more after this, I swore to myself, no more. This was the end of the line.

I needed help with the wig; I called Bettie O. Rogers, who had wigged me in Hartford when I did *False Admissions* there a month earlier, and bless her, she came down to wig me. The room was packed. I glimpsed my friend Carmine, the one who taught me Vreeland's walk, sitting ringside.

The show opened with a recording of Maria Callas singing "Vissi d'arte." A spotlight picked me out, listening to Callas. The music was supposed to fade after the first notes. The music didn't fade. It went on and on and on as I sat there like a goddamned statue. It seemed to me we heard the entire aria. But it didn't matter in the long run, because the reaction in the room was over the top. The next day I got a call from Nicky Martin.

*I*HAD KNOWN NICKY SINCE THE FIFTIES, WHEN HE WAS JOEL LEVIN-
son. He was an actor then, charming and hilarious, quipping lines
from Shakespeare to comic effect. I wanted to be his best friend. Twice
over the years we were cast in the same shows, one an ill-fated Chicago
production of *Blithe Spirit*, directed by and starring Ellis Rabb, in
which Nicky played Edith, the maid, and I played Ruth, the boring
wife. The second was Eva Le Gallienne's ill-fated Broadway production of *Alice in Wonderland*. I was the Red Queen and Nicky played the
Duck, the Dormouse, and the Train Guard. He had been teaching at
Bennington College in Vermont for a few years when he decided he
wanted to be a director. His friend Jack O'Brien had just called him.
At the time, Jack headed the Old Globe Theater in San Diego. He
knew that Nicky was trying to establish himself and asked if he had
anything he'd like to direct in the smaller theater space out there the
following season. Nicky had seen the show the night before and suggested it. It looked like we might have our first legitimate gig at the
Old Globe.

Summer 1994: *The Way of the World*

*I*N APRIL, MARK AND I WERE INVITED TO BREAKFAST WITH JACK
O'Brien. Jack is an ebullient man, very funny and sharp. Nothing
was definite, but we were hopeful. Jack called me the next day to ask if
I wanted to play Lady Wishfor't in his production of *The Way of the
World*, starting in July. Did I ever! What a role!

> *But art thou sure Sir Rowland will not fail to come? Or will a' not*
> *fail when he does come? Will he be importunate, Foible, and push?*
> *. . . I won't give him despair—but a little disdain is not amiss; a*
> *little scorn is alluring . . . yes, but tenderness becomes me best—a*
> *sort of dyingness . . . a swimmingness in the eyes . . .*

Father

Mother

The Family

Me

Hugh and MLW
Xmas in Fuchsia Moon

Brother Hugh, 21, at Princeton

Hugh and Philip Minor

Sister Taffy at 35

Upstairs at the Downstairs. Julius Monk in the driver's seat. *L. to r.* Rex Robbins, Gerry Matthews, MLW, Susan Browning, Ceil Cabot, Jack Fletcher

Dick Libertini, MLW, Paul Dooley, Jane Alexander, MacIntyre Dixon in *Twice Over Nightly*

…lius Monk Revue, 1956

…p, MLW; *right,* Jack Fletcher and
…LW (Steve Schapiro, *Life* magazine);
…ottom, l. to r. MLW, Bill Hinnant,
…at Ruhl, Gerry Matthews, Ceil Cabot,
…ordon Connell

Queen of the Industrials—The Milliken Mills Industrial Show, ca. 1960s

Volpone, Cincinnati Playhouse

MLW with husband,
Albert "Chibbie" Cibelli,
1964

Flora the Red Menace, 1965, MLW with Liza Minnelli (Photo Martha Swope)

Zan Charisse and MLW as Tessie Tura
in *Gypsy*, 1972 (Photo Martha Swope)

Joe Maher, MLW and Rosetta Lenoire, in *The Royal Family* (Photo Cliff Moore)

The Beggar's Opera,
McAlpin Theater, NYC 1971

Mary Beth Fisher and MLW in *The Birthday Party*
Huntington Theatre, Boston (Photo Gerry Goodstein)

MLW as Queen Elizabeth
with Mark Harelik,
New York Theater
Workshop 2003,
The Beard of Avon

The Way of the World, MLW as Lady Wishfor't, Old Globe Theater, San Diego, 1994

Eva Le Gallienne, Kate Burton, MLW, 1982, *Alice in Wonderland*
(Photo Martha Swope)

MLW with David Aaron Baker, Signature Theater, 1999
Bosoms and Neglect

MLW as Diana Vreeland, *Full Gallop*, 1996
(Photo Carol Rosegg)

Revival of *Cabaret*: MLW as Fräulein Schneider with Ron Rifkin, 1998

Backstage: MLW as
Mrs. Morehead, *The Women*,
Roundabout Theater, 2001

MLW as Big Edie in *Grey Gardens*, 2007
(Photo Joan Marcus)

MLW with Tony Award for Best Featured Actress
in a Musical 2007 for *Grey Gardens*

Oh, the language! And instead of the lady's maid, I was finally going to play the lady.

I adore the amount I knew before what I know today and I adore the way I got to know them. —D.V.

1977: One Day at a Time

*I*WAS THRILLED WHEN NORMAN LEAR OFFERED ME A RUNNING PART on the series *One Day at a Time*. I hadn't seen the show, I was still in *The Royal Family*, but I immediately said yes because Lear was responsible for *Mary Hartman, Mary Hartman, Maude, All in the Family*, and *The Jeffersons*, all great television comedies featuring stage actors. Lear loved stage actors. I didn't have to audition for the role, he had seen me in *Gypsy* and he just offered it.

I gave my notice at *Royal Family*, and as soon as I was out, I sat down to watch an episode of *One Day at a Time*. Actually, Denny and I sat down, smoked a joint, and watched. Our jaws dropped, slowly. Even on pot, there was not a laugh in a carload. The series was about a single mother raising two daughters. It was one of the first shows on this subject and a big hit. Lear's series were distinctive for mixing moral issues in with the comedy, issues like sexism, racism, pregnancy out of wedlock, and rape. Sometimes the fit was uncomfortable. The audience would be howling at Archie Bunker, when suddenly they heard Edith warbling that she'd almost been raped. The audience, pulled up by the shorthairs, muttered a confused, chastised, "*Ooooohhhh.*"

In the case of *One Day at a Time*, the moral issues seemed to me to far outweigh the comedy. The show had Schneider, the apartment super, played by Pat Harrington Jr., wearing a cigarette pack in his rolled up T-shirt sleeve and a toilet seat over his head, but I didn't think he was a bit funny. Oddly, offscreen he was hilarious. Real funniness in a person is something situation-comedy writers don't seem to recognize. I've seen inherently funny actors like Alice Ghostley and Leonard Frey flattened out in sitcoms. There's no room for their uniqueness. Anyway, it would be hard for Groucho Marx to be funny facing the glassy stare of the lead, Bonnie Franklin. Bonnie Franklin as mother of two teenage girls took her role as arbiter over moral issues very seriously.

Bonnie Franklin had won a Tony for her appearance in the Broadway musical *Applause*. I didn't see the show, but apparently she sang and danced on tabletops, and now she was our foremost authority on Broadway and she liked to talk about "acting beats." Having been in that world myself for some twenty years, her pronouncements on these subjects tended to add bitters to my gall.

My character was Ginny Wrobliki, cocktail waitress. I wanted to see the script before rehearsals started but was told it was under wraps until the first read-through. What the hell was in it? Atomic secrets? When we sat down around the table, I opened it and read my first line: "Hello girls." This being the first time to see them, I read the lines without much inflection. On the lunch break, the casting lady, Marion Dougherty, bustled in, took me aside, and told me the producers had caught Lear just as he was boarding a plane to tell him that I wasn't funny. He sent back a message for me, "Just yell your lines." So I yelled them for the rest of the day.

I was trapped in some kind alternative universe. Instead of increased concentration, time slowed; after the first reading, the next four days were spent in a sunny studio doing camera blocking: walk here, sit on couch, move to door, move to chair, the cast goofing their way through it. The only break in the tedium came when somebody brought in the show's weekly ratings. The cast was instantly galvanized. Everything stopped while they were pored over.

This was a four-camera show; you said your line when the red light on the camera went on. I come in the door and say "Hello girls" to camera one, and there follows a pause longer than the river Styx before the light on camera four goes on and Valerie Bertinelli says, "Hi Ginny." I was used to the George Abbott school of lickety-split delivery.

Ginny's waitress getup was a bustier, a tutu, black mesh stockings, and stiletto heels. This costume was no doubt suggested by my skimpy attire as Tessie Tura in *Gypsy*, where Lear first saw me. I look pretty cute to me now when I see re-runs, but at the time I felt utterly ridiculous.

Lear showed up for the taping of my first show. An actor I knew, Tom Lacy, was playing a sleazy rug salesman. Lear got a rubber cigar stub for him to jam in the corner of his mouth, and in a scene where we had an argument, he gave me the line, "What is that? A growth?" Huge laugh. It was the only laugh I recall getting that wasn't based on holding up a pair of pantyhose or saying, "You turkey." What was it with this "You turkey" line anyway? I was told it was a saying of the Fonz's on *Happy Days*, a big hit in the seventies.

On most theater stages the actors are not seen until the curtain rises when they are revealed as the characters they're playing. In television, just before the show begins, the cast runs out front in their bathrobes pumping their arms like prizefighters to the cheers of the audience. Then, "Places, please!" Time suddenly speeds up. A man with headphones standing next to you holding fingers in your face hisses, "Four! Three! Two! And go!" No time to think, much less clear your throat. Through the door, then "Hello girls," then all the air goes out of the balloon again waiting for camera four. Things get slower than real life.

We do two shows a night in front of two different audiences. The physical space between them and the set is filled with television cameras, cranes, and crew; they sit in bleachers watching us on suspended televisions. The shows are taped and live laughter is supplemented with canned when needed. The point is, the laughs must come at regular intervals.

We do the shows with a forty-minute dinner break in between. During dinner, any jokes that didn't get laughs are cut and we're handed rewrites. Now and then I get a laugh on a line not written to be funny, and the writers, somewhat suspicious, look at me: "Hey, you got a laugh there!"

Lear hired New York actors as guests to appear on the show every week; I greeted each one like a soul from a distant star. Mac Dixon of *Stewed Prunes* played a drunk that the daughter played by Mackenzie Phillips was trying to rehabilitate. Sitting at the breakfast table, he picked up a glass of orange juice in his violently shaking hand and the juice sloshed up into the air and hovered there for what seemed like an eternity before returning to the glass without a drop spilled. He did this not once but four times, two rehearsals and two shows. He also picked up his coffee each time with the tip of his necktie draped over the lip of the cup.

While Mac was in L.A., he looked up his idol Buster Keaton in the phone book, and there he was: "B. Keaton." He went to visit him.

I was asked several times to stay after the last show for "reaction shots." "React to what?" I barked. "Just react," they said. I didn't get it. I finally watched an episode: I'm saying my lines in my quick style and the camera is on and off me in a flash while it lingers seemingly forever on the others' faces, particularly Bonnie Franklin's. They were reacting. The whole bloody show was reacting. I can still see in my mind those interminable closeups of Bonnie Franklin's face, the Dutch-boy bob, the dimpled chin thrust up, and those tiny, slightly crossed eyes registering mild disgust.

So here I was in a show with no funny lines and no character to play. I was subletting a beige shoebox with one window overlooking Highland Avenue in West Hollywood, just down the street from where the Black Dahlia murder victim was found. I learned the hard way not to call actors I knew from New York who were living here. They were not glad to hear from me; in fact they were downright rude. Maybe it was the note of hysterical loneliness in my voice. There is no easy way, in any case, to socialize in L.A., since you have to drive miles to get anywhere, and when you get there there's no place to park.

I was weeping around the clock. I drove around in my Rent-A-Wreck VW Beetle, crying my head off. Pulling up at stoplights, drivers on either side stared in disbelief. I was weeping over the frozen-food bin in Hughes Market when an actor from New York came around the corner. "Hey! You out here, too? Isn't this great?" "Oh great! Great!" "What are you doing?" "Oh, *One Day at a Time* . . ." "Great! I'm on *All in the Family*!" "Great!!!" As soon as he disappeared I went back to weeping over the frozen food.

I felt terribly wrong to be so miserable. I knew this was the kind of break actors longed for. I saw the way people, even my own parents, reacted after seeing me on "the tube"—they didn't care about the quality of the work, I was famous! So what the hell was my problem? I couldn't fathom my own inhibition.

Aside from Lear, nobody thought I was funny. Hollywood's idea of funny wasn't mine. I felt stripped of my one strength, my one ace in the hole. To make matters worse, each character, according to the show's formula, had to have a "serious" moral dilemma at some point, and I was given some problem about an illegitimate child to work out in these embarrassingly sentimental scenes that made my bowels shrink. After a few weeks, I asked to see Lear. He sweetly took my hand and told me that when the ferociously funny stage actress Nancy Walker first started on his show *Rhoda*, she was unhappy, too, but she eventually found her sea legs.

Before coming out to L.A., I had won a lucrative four-year contract with Maxwell House Coffee playing the niece of the former Wicked Witch of the West in *The Wizard of Oz*, Margaret Hamilton.

Miss Hamilton was the official Maxwell House spokeswoman, chortling "Good to the last drop!" When she broke her hip, the sponsors cynically invented a clone niece, just in case, and I won the part by doing a perfect imitation of her. A year later, when I appeared on *One Day at a Time* dressed in a bustier, tutu, and fishnets, I was called to a meeting with a man from Maxwell House who informed me that the contract had to be terminated. My agent argued that Nancy Walker was on *Rhoda*, while simultaneously doing her Bounty paper-towel commercials in which she famously snapped, "Bounty. The quicker picker-upper." The man from Maxwell House carefully explained that coffee was not a "demonstrable" product. There was no way to show that their coffee was better than any other except through the believability of the character. I noticed that the man from Maxwell House was wearing a necktie decorated with little coffee cups spilling their last drops.

At the end of the first season of *One Day at a Time*, I came back to New York and made a lunch date with Richard, my agent. While waiting in the restaurant, I noticed a weird-looking guy in a big fuzzy hat coming through the door. He came over to the table. It was Richard. For years we had been conferring mostly by phone. Anyway, I told him how miserable I was, and he patiently explained the value of doing the show. I would come back to New York with a bigger name and be up for bigger stage roles. I took this in. He was flying to the coast the next morning to see Lear about me and another client, and he told me to think about it and let him know. Dumbbell that I was, I had not realized the effect television could have on a stage career. After mulling it over, I decided to stick with the show. I called Richard's hotel in L.A. the next evening. I forgot that it was three hours earlier out there. It was only three when he landed, and he had already seen Lear that afternoon, told him I was unhappy, and Lear, gent that he is, had released me.

I was relieved, but filled with guilt. Like a murderer. Not long ago, while brushing my teeth, it suddenly came to me what I could have played: Tessie Tura! All I had to do was play Tessie's disdain—"*I don't do no scenes. Now go screw.*" The disdain I already so deeply felt for the whole proceeding. Then I could have made music with lines like "Hello girls," or "You turkey," whatever they threw at me. But I didn't think of it. I had tortured myself and whoever else would listen, howling about having nothing to play, and the answer had been staring me in the face.

*M*AUDE WAS THE SERIES I WOULD LIKE TO HAVE BEEN ON. IT starred Bea Arthur, a woman who could make you laugh saying, "Pass the salt." I knew Bea from the old days. She had a voice like a tuba. It was a sonic boom from some underground cavern that instantly triggered hilarity in the listener. She came to a matinee of *Hot Spot*, and afterwards, sitting with her at a table within earshot of Judy Holliday's table, I asked what she thought of the show. She immediately boomed, "A faggot's fart in a windstorm."

While I was in *Gypsy*, I got a call to do a guest spot on *Maude*, which was in its first season. Because I was Angela's understudy, the producers didn't want to give me the time off, but I begged and they finally relented, and I bought them all expensive thank-you gifts, and then the call came from L.A. that they were "going in a different direction." They cast the actress Elizabeth Wilson in the guest spot instead. I was heartbroken.

Elizabeth Wilson and I could not be more different, but as far as Los Angeles was concerned, we seemed to be interchangeable.

Years later, I got a call to fly out at the last minute to replace somebody on an episode of *Maude*, and that somebody turned out to be Elizabeth Wilson. "Get that other Wilson girl!" The character was supposed to drop dead on the show, and they said Elizabeth "couldn't die funny."

At last I was going to be on *Maude*! I joked to Marion Dougherty that dropping dead didn't bode well for my future appearances on the show and she shot back, "It doesn't matter, because this is the last one."

Earnest

*I*NO SOONER ESCAPED FROM *ONE DAY AT A TIME* THAN I WENT INTO *The Importance of Being Earnest* at the Circle in the Square Theater, now uptown at 50th Street. Elizabeth Wilson, that "other Wilson girl," was Lady Bracknell and I was Prism. The beautiful Kathleen Widdoes played Cecily. Our director had a slight problem with narcolepsy. During rehearsals one day Kathleen stopped and sweetly said to him, "Steven, is there anything we could do to make you less sleepy?" We had beautiful costumes made by Ann Roth. She made me a bosom of lentil beans so that, when pressed, gave a little. Following our dress rehearsal, Circle's head Ted Mann stood up and said "Folks, I've just seen the most fabulous show,"—we all inhaled with pleasure—he continued "across the street. *Beatlemania*!"

Playing Prism after the scanty meal of Ginny Wrobliki was sheer delight. I had no scruples about emulating the great Dame Margaret Rutherford who played the part on the London stage as well as in the film. A story I heard about the stage production inspired me: apparently the director kept complaining about whispering going on during the rehearsal until it was explained to him that it was Dame Margaret sitting upstage talking to her handbag. The *Times* review of our *Earnest* opened with the line "[The director] could direct this play with his eyes closed." We posted it backstage. Kathleen and I became good friends during and after the show as Village neighbors. I loved her for her kindness, her cooking, her flaunting the rules, her playfulness. Backstage in the "voms" i.e., the dark connecting passageways underneath the seats, we enjoyed hiding and scaring the hell out of each other.

1978: *Alice* at the Public

MORE THAN ANY AUDIENCE, I DEARLY WANTED THE APPROVAL OF my fellow actors. I wanted allegiance; no upstaging, no eye crossing, no scene stealing. I imagined there was a group somewhere, a club of mutually admiring performers that excluded me.

On the other hand, I felt I could never be in their circle. I was the perpetual outsider.

In rehearsals for a production of *Alice in Wonderland* at the Public Theater, with Meryl Streep as Alice and a pride of established theater actors including Elizabeth Wilson as the White Queen, we had been coerced by the child director into weeks of improvisation; we squawked like birds and rolled around on the floor like lobsters. Crawling around on the floor caused us to become strangely vulnerable to each other. In spite of ourselves we were bound together like galley slaves. It was a reluctant intimacy. In the middle of a conversation one day, the Queen of Hearts, Olympia Dukakis, burst into tears and moaned, "I'm always alone! I'm never part of anything!" It thrilled me. Olympia was not yet a film star, but she was a busy stage actor and teacher. Her words were mine: Always alone. Separate.

We rehearsed on one whole floor of a loft building. The director sat cross-legged on the floor; she had recently had a big hit with a cast of children. Most of us were well into our middle years. I was damned if I was going to sit on the floor. There were a couple of wheeled office chairs in the loft; I commandeered one and the fine unsung actor, John Christopher Jones, got the other; I seem to recall that Chris kept his raincoat on the entire time.

I watched Meryl improvise the scene where Alice drinks from the bottle marked "drink me" and suddenly grows huge. She let out a terrifying scream, "WHAT'S HAPPENING TO ME?!" and instantly I saw the onslaught of puberty and the frightening changes that entailed.

Each day this child/director brought in a few paragraphs of Lewis Carroll's words set to a tune and played it for us to learn. There was a minor insurrection one day when some actors complained of not being singers, not being able to hit some of the notes. The director's response was to tell us that when the composer Charles Ives found a broken tuba lying under a tree, he composed music for it. Silence, then Olympia, slowly, lowly growled, "Are you saying that we are broken tubas?"

After weeks of breaking us down again and again, Joe Papp stopped by, smoked a cigar, and talked and talked. Finally, Olympia interrupted: "Joe, are you firing us?" He was. He fired us. All but Meryl and three others. Some of us were crying. Joe looked at me: "You're crying!" He was shocked. He must have thought I was a very tough broad. It was ten in the morning. We who'd been let go repaired to the bar downstairs, then Olympia walked across town to the West Village with me, buying a loaf of Zito's bread on the way. She sat in a chair in my apartment, ate the whole loaf, went into the john and threw up, then went home.

Actors are generally most friendly after the show they were in together has closed. Especially if the show was a bomb.

For a week or so after *Alice*, Elizabeth Wilson and I talked on the phone. She told me all about her sisters, her life, and I thought with pleasure, We're going to be friends! But it didn't last.

I couldn't understand it when actors were unwilling to be friendly. I took it personally. I think now the truth is there are actors who are naturally exclusive and other actors who are naturally inclusive. It's that simple.

I'm in the theater to hang out with actors. I go to the theater to see actors. They amaze me. They thrill me. I think, My God, how did they do that? A single gesture in a play can illuminate a whole world.

I once saw Nancy Walker in a production of T.S. Eliot's *The Cocktail Party*, a morbid drawing-room drama. Walker played the grande dame, the Dame Sybil Thorndike role. Seated on the sofa in her furs, her feet barely touched the floor. I was feeling bad for her, and then the butler proffered her a tray of canapés, causing her to peremptorily flip her hand at him. I gasped. That hand flip was so funny and so much bigger than the entire rest of the evening. I thought, That's what sets comedy apart from drama. It's just as real, but bigger.

You may have guessed by now that I am mad about great comediennes. Beatrice Lillie in *Ziegfeld Follies* in the fifties: the curtains opened on a seraglio; houri girls swiveled around the stage, and up in a turret stage left a tenor in a turban warbled some *Arabian Nights* ballad. Above the set was a series of arches; a few moments went by and then Miss Lillie appeared in one of the arches holding a box of Kleenex. She turned around and went back in. Moments later, she came out another arch without the Kleenex. She looked vaguely around, came down the stairs, sat down on a lounge with many pillows and started trying to arrange the pillows. There was absolutely nothing going on, but the audience was laughing hysterically. Lillie's feet were funny. At one point in *High Spirits*, the musical version of Noël Coward's play *Blithe Spirit*, she was behind a screen and the sight of her bunny slippers set the audience off.

Ruth Gordon's mouth as Dolly Levi in *The Matchmaker*, the play that became the musical *Hello, Dolly!*—those red, red lips with the lines radiating out from them were practically the heart of the play. Every time they opened, you knew another lie was about to be spoken.

An interesting side note: Nancy Walker was not a pretty woman; she was short and stocky with a horse face, but she dressed like a beautiful dame: fox furs, slinky, low-cut dresses, and fuck-me shoes.

Bea Lillie was dapper and immaculate, her hair perennially pulled back into a toque.

Once on the lingerie floor of Saks Fifth Avenue, waiting for the elevator, I noticed this chic little woman standing next to me. She was humming. She turned and smiled a little closed-mouth smile at me.

That mouth! Ruth Gordon! Another not-beautiful actress beautifully dressed. She loved clothes so much she wrote about them in her memoirs. I get that.

More Hugh

*B*Y THE LATE 1970S HUGH WAS CHAIRMAN OF THE ENGLISH DEPART-ment at Wagner College and he and Phyllis lived together. They were married for about ten minutes in the early sixties and then divorced, and then a few years later he moved into her 12th Street apartment and they stayed together for the rest of their lives. He never pretended he wasn't gay—one of his most attractive traits was his lack of pretense—he never had a boyfriend; sex was always with strangers.

On weekends in Connecticut, I socialized with their circle of married couples, me the odd woman out. The scales fell from my eyes one night at a dinner party. We were all pretty squiffed. Instead of my wonderful brother, I suddenly saw a fat-bellied, pontificating old fool. He was starting to look and sound like Mummy. When he began to aim thinly veiled insults at a houseguest of mine, I told him to shut up. "What?" he said.

"I said shut up."

He then hauled off and socked me in the eye. This was the fight we should have had when we were kids. He called up the next day abject, apologizing, but I told him I couldn't be around him anymore. I knew, dimly, that I had to break away. He was very angry. I was now the enemy. We stopped speaking for several years. Eventually I sold the Connecticut house and moved to an old farmhouse in upstate New York.

Weird fact: We lived next door to each other in the country and in the city. All during the years we were estranged, I heard him yawn every morning through the apartment wall.

1981: *Fools*

*F*OOLS IS ABOUT STUPID PEASANTS, AND PROBABLY THE ONLY PLAY of Neil Simon's I rarely hear mentioned. It's very funny, but it bombed, I think, because his audience, upper-class New Yorkers, couldn't identify with retarded peasants. I read for the stupid wife. This was the rare occasion when an audition went well: my stupid husband ordered me to "lower my voice" and I instantly bent my knees, which delighted Neil. The stupid husband was played by Harold Gould, a wonderfully eccentric actor; in rehearsals he was forever trying to work out the illogic of these peasants, muttering to the air, "If I wash my face with fish, then I would probably use fish to clean my shoes," etc.

Neil Simon was fun to watch during rehearsals. He sat along the wall looking into the distance, his lips moving, testing out funny lines. If Neil Simon could have his way, his actors would not move. He felt any action was a distraction from his lines. He even complained about the set being too distracting: "It looks like a gingerbread house," he moaned. I had a Hula-Hoop in my skirt that drove him mad.

There were problems with the script, and at some point Mike Nichols was brought in to fix things. There were scenes in the play when Gould had a funny line or action and my character had no response. Gould at one point shut the door in my face, and my response as given in the script was simply to re-enter. Since everything these characters did was counterintuitive, I decided to pull the door instead of push, and finally climb in through the transom. Neil hated it but Mike loved it. Each day as we rehearsed the rewrites, he gave me more and more funny things to do. Once during this period, Mike pulled me under the backstage stairs and whispered, "I adore you." Naturally, I was thrilled out of my mind. I looked up and my erstwhile friend Pamela Reed who played the ingénue was standing there watching us. She grabbed me: "What did he tell you?" Like an idiot I told her, and the next day with everybody onstage she called to Mike, "Hey Mike, who else do you adore?"

141

It was thrilling to be directed by Mike Nichols; he came out with these insights in rehearsals that illuminated everything. And the best thing about him was his love of funny women.

1982: *Zelig*

I'M PRETTY SURE NICHOLS SUGGESTED ME TO WOODY ALLEN TO play his evil sister in *Zelig*. I didn't get a script; Allen was famous for not letting anybody see his scripts, but then, I didn't have any lines.

Before filming began, I was called in for a costume check. The genius Santo Loquasto was doing the costumes. I may not have had lines, but I had an extensive wardrobe. This test day I was put into an outfit and taken up some stairs to a makeup room for Allen's approval. Allen was sitting in the makeup chair, watching a ballgame on television. When he turned to check out my outfit, half his face was black with big lips and bushy black brows. I went away, put on another costume, and came back. This time he was putty-faced with Asian eyes. I couldn't control myself, I burst out laughing. I learned later that *Zelig* was about a man who turned into whomever he was with; if he was introduced to an African-American he turned into an African-American, if he was with an Asian, etc. I played his evil sister and was seen with him in countless newsreel shots.

On the first day of shooting, Allen turned to me and said, "Don't act!" I shot back, "Don't worry!" And that was about the extent of our conversation. Over the next couple of months, I climbed in and out of several Hispano-Suizas with him without exchanging a word. Now and then an inadvertent giggle escaped me. Nerves.

There were a lot of crowd scenes in *Zelig*. One day, the streets of Bensonhurst were teeming with Hasidim in black hats, and the next day they were filled with Nazi soldiers. It was like living inside a Woody Allen dream. One location was the enormous lobby of an old movie palace in some outer borough. I was costumed and told to wait. Hours went by; I fell asleep on somebody's coat in a van. Around 3 A.M., I was shaken awake and escorted into the theater. The lobby was jammed with two hundred extras in evening wear, and every single one of them was holding a lit cigarette.

When I wasn't in the shot, there was no designated place to hang out other than the street. One day the crowd was milling around in drab thirties costumes when the lunch break was called, and a guy on a dolly high above us with a bullhorn started yelling: "Move back against the wall! Back against the wall!" He was trying to get the principals in line before the extras, but it felt a bit too reminiscent of another time. I was also in a drab thirties getup, and when the bullhorn tried to herd me back with the crowd I barked, "I am not an extra!" It sounded in my ears like, "I am not a Jew!"

Fortunately, I knew the makeup lady, Fern, from another job. Fern and Romaine, the hair lady, rescued me. Fern and Romaine were known as the Lettuce Sisters. They let me hang out in their trailer and filled me in on the script.

Another time we were in a holding area in a school basement in some suburb, when I looked across the room and saw Hitler sitting there. Suddenly he saw me and, waving excitedly, shouted, "Mary Lou-eese! Hi!"

1982: *Whorehouse*

UNDOUBTEDLY THE STANDOUT FOR LOUSY FILM EXPERIENCES WAS *The Best Little Whorehouse in Texas*. I was hired for three days' work on location in Edna, Texas. I had just finished playing a featured role on Broadway, so perhaps I went down there with a slightly inflated level of self-worth. I was to play a nervous townswoman in one big scene.

The actors were put up in a motel on a lone stretch of highway about an hour and forty minutes from the set. This was Texas; from motel to set we drove past one man's ranch the whole way. I was picked up at dawn and sent to Hair and Makeup's trailer, and as soon as I got in the chair a production assistant popped a head in and barked, "Mary? They need you on the set in five minutes." Hair wound my locks into a Leaning Tower of Pisa and Makeup dabbed on eyes and mouth and I went to the set.

The scene I was in was with Burt Reynolds, Jim Nabors, and a stunt mule. The mule was supposed to sit on the hood of a car. We rehearsed; I had studiously practiced my Texas accent, but after standing next to Jim Nabors for five minutes, it reverted to a Jim Nabors accent. It didn't really matter because we didn't shoot the scene that day, or for the next two weeks, because either the sun would go behind a cloud or the mule would refuse to sit on the car or Burt would refuse to come out of his big black trailer. Every morning, I was called to the set at six and hurried through hair and makeup, and then they moved to another shot and I spent the rest of the day standing on the sidewalk in the blazing heat with this ridiculous hairdo among a crowd of onlookers who took me for one of their own. The alternative was to sit in my "trailer," which was more like an air-conditioned coffin. Young girls had come from miles around to catch a glimpse of Burt. One I talked to was determined to somehow smuggle herself into Burt's trailer and go away with him. She might have done, for all I know.

This went on for thirteen days; twelve nights spent in a motel room with nothing to read or drink. Morning after morning, as I sat down in the makeup chair, tears rolled uncontrollably down my face. The makeup man dabbed at my cheeks and patted my shoulder.

The entire set was in an ugly mood, from the top down to the production assistants, who yelled at us like we were cattle. Maybe they were hired cowhands, but someone was treating *them* like shit. One night, as a van full of actors pulled away from the set, Dom DeLuise stuck his bare behind out a window and mooned the crew.

144

I was finally released without shooting the scene. A month later I was flown out to Hollywood, where Burt and Jim and I filmed it in a back lot, sans mule.

1980s: Mega-Agents

*I*T SEEMS TO ME THE FEW TIMES I EVER ATTEMPTED TO PROMOTE myself were doomed to failure. A fortyish actress I knew had managed to get herself on talk shows by proclaiming that she had chosen to be celibate. Never mind that the only way a woman in her forties gets laid is by tying herself to railroad tracks—it got her on talk shows. This wouldn't have worked for me. But in 1980, as I was going directly from Ellis Rabb's *Philadelphia Story* at Lincoln Center to Neil Simon's *Fools* on Broadway and getting film work all in one season, I imagined that I was moving to a higher place in the pecking order, and consequently required better representation.

The eighties was the era of big shoulder pads and celebrity agents like David Geffen and Sue Mengers. This was when meeting an agent he gave you his résumé rather than the other way around. I had been with Richard, one man in a one-room office in the Steinway Building on West 57th Street, for fifteen years. I wince now to think of my disloyalty, but I dumped him for a fancy mega-agency called Triad, recommended by my erstwhile friend Pamela Reed.

The day I signed with Triad I was ushered into a room to meet their "people." They sat in a circle around me smiling, expectant. I was back in the high school principal's office. What was I supposed to do? I had no ability to schmooz. It had not occurred to me before that personal charisma had anything to do with an actor's success. In the silence that ensued, the agency head quietly informed me that they were not averse to letting actors go if the fit wasn't right. In other words, the shoe was now on the other foot.

There was no fax, and no email then; actors had to go to the office to pick up their "sides," or audition script bits. The reception room featured unborn-calf-leather sofas and a giant slab of granite on which sat a six-foot floral display. The receptionist was a bored young man in Armani and a string of pearls. When asked for a script, he gestured languidly to a cardboard box on the floor, which I had to squat down and scrabble through to find my four lines.

There was one good egg there, Joanna Ross, who did what she could for me. I was happy when I heard she quit and moved to Italy with her husband and child. They bought an old house and I heard they made their own olive oil.

Being Packaged

*T*HIS WAS MY FIRST EXPERIENCE WITH BEING "PACKAGED." THE agency sold a star to a film along with other clients in smaller roles. I found myself being shoehorned into "woman on the telephone" roles. There were four or five years of no work except for these filmettes. They were usually already in production, and I would arrive at some bleak motel off a thruway with instructions to stay in my room and wait for the call to the set. "Six A.M. call, Mary." (Evidently the part was too small to warrant learning my full name.) "Be in the lobby at five A.M. for pickup." Once on the set, the actors and crew, having been together for months, indulged in an easy camaraderie over and around my head.

At the same time I was trying not to meet the eager glances of the people commonly known as "extras," but officially referred to as "background." I was invariably seated among the "background" in church pews or courtrooms, my two lines a skimpy dress separating me from them, and I was desperate not to be seen as one of them. While I was busy ignoring them, the stars were often doing the same to me.

Some of the films I had teensy parts in over the years were *Up the Sandbox, Teachers, The Money Pit, King of the Gypsies, Pet Sematary, The Adventures of Huck Finn, Mr. Wonderful, Everybody Wins,* and *Stepmom.* Some of these films didn't even make it to the big screen. They went straight to the video store, back when there were video stores. In *Stepmom* I only had three lines, but for some reason my billing was enormous. Ingmar Bergman's cinematographer, Sven Nykvist, worked on *King of the Gypsies.* I only had a few lines here, too, but I had some great close-up shots. In *Mr. Wonderful,* my part was one scene where I performed a trick at a company dinner of removing my bra while remaining fully clothed. I played a granny in Stephen King's *Pet Sematary.* I didn't want to do it; I had been offered Lady Bracknell in *The Importance of Being Ernest* in Baltimore, but they kept coming back with more and more money until I succumbed. Now some twenty years later, though you'd be hard put to find me in that film, I'm still receiving hefty residual checks.

A side note on the background in *Pet Sematary:* in the church funeral scene, the pews were filled with local townspeople playing local townspeople. In this scene, the little white coffin of the demon infant gets jostled, and a tiny arm falls out, whereupon everybody reacts. I couldn't believe the wailing and screaming and tearing of bodices of these people. In take after take, as that little arm fell out of the coffin again and again, I was finding it very hard to sustain a look of horror, much less keep myself from ogling them as they went crazy again and again, groaning, keening, real tears flowing down their cheeks, pounding their fists on their heads, throwing themselves on the floor.

The irony didn't escape me that I was making good money from these jobs. This was at a time when residuals paid handsomely: foreign rights, television rights. The more the checks poured in, the more depressed I got, not doing anything that made me feel like an actor.

Green Card

*I*HAD A SLIGHTLY BETTER ROLE IN *GREEN CARD*. BUT IN A SCENE with Gérard Depardieu, I was surprised when the camera was turned to face me that he stayed put, sitting on a box next to the camera, to do his lines with me. I still anticipated being invisible to him as we sat waiting for lights, camera, action, so I kept my head down, but Depardieu was having none of this; I think he felt ignored. He took to muttering the titles of films he had been in. I wasn't familiar with them; each night after work I went to the video store and rented *Get Out Your Handkerchiefs*, *The Last Metro*, and *Going Places*. They were terrific films. I came back the next day and told him how much I loved each one. He was happy.

Nonprofit Theaters

*I*N THE EIGHTIES I STARTED TO AUDITION FOR THESE NONPROFIT off-Broadway theater companies: Manhattan Theater Club, Playwrights Horizons, and Second Stage. The people who ran them all seemed to be young, upper-class preppies; the plays they produced seemed to be mainly about people like themselves: young, upper-class preppies. The actors' salaries were laughable. It was a whole new scene. I couldn't get over it, I took enormous umbrage to all of it. But at this point in my life I was taking umbrage to everything. I was filled with resentment and terribly lonely. The thing I loved most about being in the theater was being part of a family and going out drinking with everybody after the show. But for a quite a while now, when the curtain came down the other actors were going home to their own families. I was going home to drink myself to sleep. I had been drinking myself to sleep every night for the past thirty years.

My drink of choice was wine. I ran out one day. I was in my house upstate, and didn't feel like driving all the way back to town, so I went to bed without drinking. I didn't buy a bottle the next day so didn't drink that night or the night after that and in that way without making a conscious decision I stopped drinking altogether. A year later, almost to the day, I was "slipped a micky," as W.C. Fields would have put it—a waiter innocently put a jigger of vodka in my grapefruit juice—and that scared me so much I started going to AA. It took years for my outlook to change, but it did. Eventually.

Fired

*A*ROUND THIS TIME I CALLED MY AGENCY AND SOMEONE FROM William Morris answered the phone. Morris had swallowed Triad, and a few of their clients had been spit out along the way, including myself. It frightened me not to have anybody looking out for me, even though they were lousy at it, but by this time I was too deeply invested in the Vreeland play to care too much. And I pretty quickly found another agency, a small one, to take me on.

November 1994: *Full Gallop* with the Allens

*B*Y JUNE, NO DATE FOR OUR PLAY AT THE OLD GLOBE HAD BEEN set, but we were hopeful. We were working on the script at my house upstate when I got a phone call from the producer, Lewis Allen, who said he and his wife were interested in producing it on Broadway. Lewis's wife, Jay Presson Allen, was the writer of the stage adaptations of Muriel Spark's *The Prime of Miss Jean Brodie* and Truman Capote's *Tru*, two very successful Broadway plays. Lewis said they'd heard talk about our Vreeland play at a dinner party and they wanted to meet with us. A Broadway production! Money! A sumptuous set! Real peonies and parrot tulips and forced quince! We sent a script to them and in a few days it was arranged that we would meet for lunch at Fred's, Barney's chic restaurant.

Jay Presson Allen, a rangy, imperious Texan, did all the talking, regaling us with stories of her derring-do. She reported with glee how she got even with a guy she didn't like by dragging her car key along the flank of his brand-new Mercedes. She told us how she couldn't get Bobby Morse to stop crying during rehearsals of *Tru*, what a pain in the ass he was crying all the time, she wanted to fire him. She informed us that our script was "almost there." "It's almost there, it just needs one more thing, one more little something to make it click. But don't look at me to fix it," she warned. "I have no intention of doing any writing on it myself!" As if I was itching for her to get her paws on my baby.

In July I went out to do *The Way of the World*. When I got back in September, Mark and I met again with the Allens and Jack O'Brien at the Four Seasons Brasserie, a gay, laughing affair, though nothing was firmly stated as far as I could tell. Finally, we got the word: *Full Gallop* was set to be staged at the Old Globe Blackbox Theater in December.

Two days before leaving town, Jay Allen suggested that she, Mark, and I meet to "workshop" the script. Mark tape-recorded the session. She had a lot of ideas, and I wanted to be open to them, but I was aware of a wall going up inside me. Mark, on the other hand, was growing increasingly jubilant with her every word. She suggested that Vreeland should call Swifty Lazar a "little Jew." "Add some shock to the mix!" "Yes!" shouted Mark. Then she said why not have Vreeland lift her pant leg above her knee, plop her eyeglassses on it, and say, "This is what Swifty looks like." "Yes!" shouted Mark again. It was obvious he was captivated. This was almost the end of the fifth year of working on the script, rearranging, refining, re-refining it. And I was starting rehearsals in two days.

When somebody asked who Jay Allen was, some wag replied, "A Park Avenue matron who says 'fuck' a lot."

The smaller stage at the Old Globe was an awkward round with audience seating on three sides. I wondered how the hell I would be able to sit on a sofa and talk to three sides. I decided there would be a couple maiden aunts who sat upstage left and right. It wasn't much help, but it was all I could come up with. On top of this, I would be obliged to make my entrance down a long stairway.

The first night I arrived, Nicky and I met with the set designer over dinner. He sat silent, his eyes bugging as we babbled away, describing Vreeland's Garden in Hell. We didn't see him again. He skipped town. The next day I got a load of what had been dragged up from the theater's storeroom: fumed oak bureaus and chairs suitable for a production of *The Wild Duck*. I looked at Nicky; Nicky is, if nothing else, the consummate home decorator. His Village apartment was done to perfection in French Provincial: touches of red, lots of toile, and tasteful objets d'art, books, photos, and mementos up the wazoo. "Nicky," I said. "Look at this furniture. Is there a single piece here that you would put in your living room?" He got the point. The set became somewhat more elegant, somewhat more red, but in the end it was still nowhere near her Garden, or anybody's garden. I mean, God, there were no walls!

Theaters

THEATER IN THE ROUND IS A PIG IN A POKE. IT'S A MONEY-SAVING device that goes along with the demise of a separate entrance for actors and that lovely old fixture, the stage doorman. You make your way to and from backstage through the lobby so there's no way to avoid audience members you may not want to see. In *Blithe Spirit* in Chicago, when Jean Marsh as Elvira the ghost waited for her entrance cue at the top of the aisle of the McCormick Place theater in the round, in her mauve ghost makeup specially sent for from New York and her mauve gown and mauve nail polish on her bare feet, couples came up to her and handed her their tickets.

The de Lys was a musty old house when I was there years ago. It had rats. It probably still does. But that stage, deep and wide, is still an ideal playing area, in perfect relation to the orchestra and the balcony. This is not often the case. I've played in huge old theaters with cavernous orchestra pits yawning between stage and first row, obliging the actors to come down to act on the lip, leaving the furniture upstage. I once played in a space that doubled as a soup kitchen with plastic chairs arranged in a circle where the actors were directed to stand or sit according to sight lines. The Cincinnati Playhouse stage is edged with a cement moat you have to keep one eye on at all times to avoid falling into it. Most non-proscenium stages are all too comfortably within reach of the front row, so you have to die or cry while stepping over feet, programs, coats, and the occasional sleeping head. There's the present-day Circle in the Square which, unlike the original Circle with its gently sloping benches and broad playing area, really ought to be called the Tongue in the Groove. The stage is a gulch, a crevasse between towering cliffs of audience members who have an excellent view of each other while the actor below has no place to stand without blocking himself and/or his fellow actor.

The rehearsal space can be hell as well. In rehearsals for *Who's Afraid of Virginia Woolf* at the Geva Theater in Rochester, there was a wide column, apparently load-bearing, dead center of George and Martha's living room. We had to peer around it to insult the guests.

1984-1985: On the Road Again

*I*N THE LATE EIGHTIES I WENT ON TWO ROAD TOURS: *THE ODD COU-ple (Female Version)*, with those incomparable comediennes Rita Moreno and Sally Struthers; and *Social Security*, with that great theatrical duo, Lucie Arnaz and Larry Luckinbill.

I wasn't nuts about signing on for a three month tour in *The Odd Couple*, but I was newly sober and raw, stripped of my cover. I badly needed to be needed somewhere. It was only winter stock, and it would get me through the holidays. This was 1984. The director was Neil Simon's brother, Danny. I had a history with Danny. He was a director on television's Alan King Show in the Seventies. I was playing the Girl in the Owl Coat in Neil's *Promises, Promises* when I was told that I was to be on the show. Apparently whenever Danny needed an extra woman he just called Neil and they sent over whomever was playing the Girl in the Owl Coat; like takeout.

The lines in the script read, "Anne," "Jimmy," "Jerry," "Woman." "Woman" was me. In the first sketch I was "Woman in hair curlers." In those days, it was essential that funny women wear hair curlers. They had to look like hell. The rumpled writers, coughing, smoking, looking like they slept under a truck, argued: "It's funny if she gets the pie in her face and then falls down," "No, no, no, it's funnier if she falls down first, then gets the pie in her face!"

The one redeeming thing about this experience was meeting the guest star. Lena Horne! She was relaxed and chatty. She watched horror movies on late night television and every morning she asked me if I saw the one the night before. "The man eats people's brains! He loves to eat brains!" The night of the actual show, instead of her dressing room she changed in the wardrobe room next to the set. The wardrobe women wrapped a sari around her, she slid a bracelet up her arm, the double doors opened, and she glided out, hit her mark, and sang her first note just as the orchestra began.

The Odd Couple jokes were pretty hoary. Mickey the Cop, my part, had one joke about my husband lashing me to the bedpost with my handcuffs. Rita Moreno and Sally Struthers were Florence (Felix) and Olive (Oscar). Rita was dark and skinny and Sally was plump and rosy in her matching flowered outfits and permed mass of blonde curls. It wasn't clear to me who played which. The other poker players, Renee, Vera, and Sylvie, were played by a Sexpot, a Butterball, and a Behemoth, in that order. Every morning, the Behemoth barged into rehearsals, slapped a purse the size of Romania down on the table, and hijacked the conversation.

Odd Couple Diary

*F*IRST READ-THROUGH: THE LAUGHTER IS DEAFENING. HUGE GUF- faws, table poundings, thigh-slappings. "Oh, oh, my eyes! I'm laughing so hard I can't see!" "I don't know how I'm going to get through this night after night!"

Danny to the Sexpot: I want you to change the way you do your lines.

SP: What do you mean?

D: It's not funny. Cut the whiney stuff. Come on stronger.

SP: Wait a minute. I'm not computing this.

D: Don't do this: (*imitates*) "Whaa whaa whaa." Be strong. Come on stronger. Say the lines.

SP: Wait. (*in tears*) Give me a minute.

D: I will if you'll come over to my hotel room and give me a massage.

SP: (*smashes fist into wall*) I'm totally confused now.

D: What's the matter? I'm just telling you you're not funny this way.

SP: Can I—I need a couple of minutes.

D: Okay, if we can have sex first. Everybody leave the room.

Rita sidles by: Hey people, we gotta nip this in the bud.

It dawned on me that we have been hired for our funny voices. The Sexpot has a husky rasp, the Butterball gurgles, the Behemoth honks, and I figure I was chosen for my bark.

When we finally get on our feet, it is a question who was directing. "Wait, wait!" Sylvie the Behemoth honks. "She should come around this way and hold onto me—and then I'll come in like this and grab at her and then she'll say her line!" And Danny says, "Great!" It's komedy with a K. Vera the Butterball sidles up to me and gurgles, "Oy."

On the ten-minute breaks, Sylvie throws a massive arm over the little man's shoulders and marches him into corners for confabs. He looks like her lunch.

I long to escape. I'm very worried about my cat City Kitty now. I think I will be able to take him with me on tour, but the stage manager Marty sniffs: "Not possible."

Our first stop is Dallas. The bus pulls up in front of the hotel and the company explodes through the doors, pushing and shoving to get to the desk first; "I can't be above the second floor." "I have to have a nonsmoking room." "I need light. I have to have a lot of light." They roar to the elevators; the doors closes, the elevators rise, then just as the second group is up at the desk, the elevators start back down again. The first group swarms out and shoves through: "There was a smoker in my room!" "The room you gave me is brown! It has brown walls!"

Downtown Dallas is a maze of Ozymandian edifices, banks bigger than St. Peter's and twice as high. I had packed all seven volumes of *Remembrance of Things Past*. I planned to spend the next three months reading Proust, but after a week of hotel food—chicken stuffed with shrimp and beef balls in cream sauce with two string beans—I started spending all my free time searching for broccoli. I'm a mad woman scuttling through black glass canyons, muttering, "Where the hell is some broccoli?" There are no little places tucked up side streets, there are no side streets; just ramps onto freeways looping into the distance.

We open and everybody is jumping up and down, hugging, fist-pumping: "We did it!" "They loved us!" "We're a hit! We're a hit!" Trudging to our dressing rooms, Butterball grunts, "We'll see." Manny Azenberg the producer, Neil, and the odious Marty are in a huddle backstage.

Next morning I come down for breakfast, and the only other person in the dining room is Danny. "Mind if I give you your notes now? Wait for that laugh after Sylvie says her line about the hotel, and when you get up to move her chair and say that line about the chair, there's a laugh there. You're not getting the laugh when she crosses to you with the phone, you have to say it louder and you'll get the laugh. In the second act you girls get a big laugh when . . ."

Arriving at the theater for rehearsal an hour later, Danny is nowhere to be seen. Marty informs us that from now on Neil will be our director. Neil has fired his own brother!

Downtown Houston is another city suffering from gigantism with musical fountains. A couple of us are in the wardrobe room complaining about getting scurvy from lack of fresh vegetables when the wardrobe mistress, something of a bank building herself, drawls, "Ya'll want some good home cookin'?" We leap into her white Cadillac Seville, swoop onto the freeway, and eventually pull up to a cinderblock building. The mistress says this was where the "blue hairs" ate. Inside, television screens quoting scripture run along the wall; piled on hot tables beneath them, miles and miles of God's real, fresh, home-cooked food. Roast beef, ham, chicken, turkey, corn, carrots, beets, squash, beans, beets, potatoes, cabbage, collards, spinach, tomatoes, and broccoli! Everything cooked three ways, plus cakes, cookies, puddings, and pies. We take two of everything.

Neil is not a people person. He writes brilliant dialogue and he doesn't want actors fucking it up by acting. He proceeded to read his director notes to the cast and managed to insult just about everybody. He skips the custom of giving the stars their notes in private; Rita is fuming and Sally is crying.

Sitting at the poker table night after night, the Behemoth's giant mandibles are everywhere at once, slapping cards around, tossing chips hither and yon, thighs jiggling belowdecks. Physical business is surreal: I cringe upstage, Vera totters, squealing in the path of a maddened dirigible, throwing furniture out of her way. *Bang! Crash! Oof!*

The only really funny people in the show are the pinch hitters for the Pigeon sisters, played by Lewis J. Stadlen and this adorable kid in his first Broadway role, Tony Shalhoub.

I am having a session with my therapist on a pay phone nailed to a post on a sandy backstreet, sobbing and wailing about my stupid life, my mother, and this guy comes along, leans up against a fence and lights up. I signal I'll be off in a minute, he shrugs, I go back to wailing.

Rumors of rewrites are relayed to us through Rosencranz the stage manager: "I spoke to Neil, he's completely rewritten the first act, you know. Oh yeah, you're not going to be playing poker any more. You're going to be playing Trivial Pursuit!" Another step backward for womankind.

I call home. The guy watching City Kitty changed his name to Sydney.

We spend Christmas in Palm Beach: tinsel in the Palm court; the Behemoth bawling "Little Drummer Boy" off-key, and ordering us to join in.

On the Road (Again) '84–'85

I'VE BECOME OBSESSED WITH LIVING ARRANGEMENTS. WE'RE BEING put in some unbelievable dumps. In Fort Lauderdale it was a motel on a landspit between two freeways and my dank room had wall-to-wall purple shag that had God knows what in it. I went looking and found this adorable little cottage on a sleepy back road. It has louvered glass windows on three sides. I can't believe my luck. It's like something out of *The Postman Always Rings Twice*.

I've been told to keep all the louvers shut up tight when I'm out because of the high crime rate. This means coming home to the inside of a toaster oven, but I can at least keep the windows open to the cooling night breezes while I sleep.

Last night I woke up to the most horrendous noise. This sleepy back road turns out to be a drag strip; all night long jalopies roared by inches from my pillow. Fume from hot throttles filled my nose.

I have moved to a motel near the beach. The room has windows overlooking a canal with a sign reading: CAUTION: MANATEE.

I thought this place had a kind of rustic charm until I moved in and realized it's just rust. The pots and pans, the stove, the fridge, the forks and knives, the coat hangers, the television set, everything is covered in rust.

Today I found some Chopin on my little radio! I fixed a glass of Coke over ice and sat down with *Swann's Way* and when I picked up the glass it dripped on the radio and killed it.

In Orlando we're in one of those ubiquitous apartment complexes featuring coffin-shaped rooms with one heavily draped window overlooking trash bins. We're in the middle of nowhere—no stores, not even sidewalks. I suddenly became frantic for a *New York Times*. I rented a car and drove to the nearest mall and to my utter delight, spotted a *Times* machine! I dropped in eight quarters and got two tissue-thin pages of "Business and Sports." Just as I was about to start weeping I spotted a bookstore! A bookstore! I went in and prowled up and down the aisles, there was nothing but bodice-rippers and bibles. But then just as I was stomping out I spotted a *New Yorker*. Saved! I drove back to the room, got into bed and opened it. It was three months old. I'd already read it.

There has never been anything like that I've ever seen with my eyes that had such a quality of total aban-donola! —D.V.

L.A.

IN L.A. I'VE BEEN ABLE TO RENT A LOVELY HOUSE IN LAUREL Canyon. It has a wall of glass that slides open and connects the living room to the terrace.

I've been told that because of the Manson murders the glass wall needs to be closed and locked at night. There are no other windows in the house, so I sleep in an airless vacuum.

The burglar alarm has to be turned on when I go out. The burglar alarm is made of rubber. It has many rubber buttons, which I haven't quite mastered. I try, God knows; I want to be thoroughly responsible. Today, halfway down Laurel Canyon, I realized I'd set the alarm but had forgotten to close the glass wall. Traffic down this endlessly winding road was bumper to bumper. Any thought of doing a U-turn was out of the question, so I left it all day and when I got back everything was fine. I suspect the rubber alarm is a fake.

Another reason I have to keep the wall shut is coyotes. When I told the company hairdresser that I'd had my cat, City Kitty, flown out to me, he became hysterical about coyotes. He said one had just killed his friend's cockapoo in that same canyon. So much for easy living in the sunshine state nowadays.

In St. Petersburg, we are all in a huge pink palazzo. Right on the beach. There is a pool and parasailing. Crumbling decor inside, long smelly hallways. The dining room lined with Red Skelton's original clown paintings. I love my tower room. My window looks out on blank blue sky. I am looking and am startled when this big blonde dolly drifts into view, so close I could have reached out and touched her. It was Sally Struthers, arms and legs sticking straight out, parasailing.

Reading *Swann's Way* in bed in Baltimore, I come across Madame Verdurin, vulgar, overbearing, telling everybody where to sit and what to do. I am thrilled to recognize the Behemoth! Why is this such a pleasure? Everything is explained. Madam V plays her idea of a great society hostess, determined to climb to the top. Sylvie after sitting in a hot tub in LA. for the past twenty years is suddenly a Broadway insider as she strides the halls honking, "The nut is up! The nut is up!"

In Baltimore, Manny Azenberg tells us he had "very exciting news." The tour will be extended another three months. A voice in the ranks mutters, "There goes my marriage." After Washington there will be a three-week break for rewrites, then back into re-hearsals with a new director and then to L.A for a month!! My heart is sinking. No way to jump ship. No unemployment benefits if you quit. We are headed for Broadway. Manny keeps saying, "Nothing's engraved in stone!" but it feels like a gravestone to me. This is just supposed to get me through the holidays. What is the alternative? No work, sitting upstate freezing in snow, nobody around. If I walk, I will be demonized by Neil and my agents, who, as it is, treat me like crap.

The *Washington Post* said that I was the only person onstage who appeared to be acting. Uh-oh. When I come down the hall, all the dressing room doors are closed. I hear hissing. I had been hearing hiss-ing for a while now. Like an over-zealous radiator. It's coming from Vera's room, a long string of "she's," "she's," "she's," "she says," "she's so," "she's such," a perpetual, paranoia-induced hiss.

We wait onstage after the final curtain to meet our new director, Gene Saks. I knew Gene when he was Bea Arthur's husband. Pep talk. Applause.

In rehearsals in New York, Gene is giving me funny bits, throwing me a nickel here, a dime there. Each time he does, Rita wails, "Ohhhhh, that's so fun-ee!"

In notes session each night after the show in L.A. Gene cuts a funny bit he gave me, one by one, until they are all cut. I keep asking why, he just looks sheepish, but then Gene always looks sheepish. He has no reason he can give me.

In the hall backstage in L.A., Manny, Neil, and Gene—tanned, tailored, middle-aged producer, writer and director stand with their new young wives genially conferring with each other while rheumy coughs issue from the dressing rooms of six middle-aged, worn-out actresses.

Except for *Promises, Promises,* this is the only long run on Broadway I had ever been in. It ran for 295 performances. I lasted three months. Every day on the way to the theater, I remind myself how great it was to have steady work, but every day as I stepped through the stage door, I entered a decompression chamber. Nobody talking, nobody having any fun, just the sound of hissing behind closed doors.

1990

WHEN I HEARD THAT HUGH HAD CONTRACTED AIDS I ASKED my sister's son Duncan, who was close to him, to keep me posted on what was happening. When he went into the hospital I went to see him. The disease had hit his brain. He was sitting up in bed babbling, but some part of him knew what was happening. He was eating everything on his plate. He mumbled, "Got to build myself up." He was going into the hall and buying candy from the machine. On my next visit I brought him a mango. He bit into it, the juice rolled down his chin. He mumbled "It's delishush." A wave of gratitude went through me. I felt as if for the first time in our lives he was allowing me to give him something. After two weeks in the hospital he was moved to a hospice. As he wrestled with the nurse who was trying to get him into his bed he roared, "Unhand me, woman!" The nurse said these were his last words.

All his life he desperately wanted respectability. I found it so strange that this cultured, eccentric man, a PhD and member of MENSA, should want nothing more at the end of his life than to have his name in the New York Social Register. He wrote letters to them but received no answer.

Full Gallop

Mark arrived in San Diego with script changes he had made with Jay Allen. He showed up at the theater and tried to give them to Nicky Martin. I was outraged. I told him I was not having this and to go away, and after that, Nicky obliged me by barring Mark from rehearsals. He didn't go home, he stayed out there.

I didn't want to have anything to do with Mark at this point. He was having a lark, driving to L.A. in an upgraded rental convertible while I was hard at work rehearsing and learning how to make an entrance down a flight of stairs. One day he accosted me in the parking lot. As I was getting into my car, he screamed: "If you weren't half a millionaire you'd be in an insane asylum!" It really hurt to be screamed at, but at the same time it struck me as hilarious. Sometimes at the most serious moments . . .

It was announced that the Allens were coming out to see the show. I was still hoping they would produce it "as is."

We four met, and again Jay Allen told me she had no intention of writing it herself, that it only needed "one more little thing to make it work." Then she said Vreeland should talk to Reed, her dead husband. I relented, wrote something along the lines of, "Oh, Reed, I do miss you! You were such a picker-upper, blah blah blah." I felt like Dolly Levi in *The Matchmaker*. I was embarrassed by it, it was so out of character.

I don't know how I got through this run. Well, I do. The sheer pleasure of rolling Vreeland's words out. All the rest was up for grabs.

Nicky's William Morris agent, Gilbert Parker, came out to see the show. Parker seemed to handle all the working directors and playwrights in town, he was a direct conduit to off-Broadway theater companies like Manhattan Theater Club, Playwrights Horizons, and Second Stage. And Parker adored Nicky. So William Morris became our agent for *Full Gallop*. I have often thought that without Nicky's adorableness, we might never have seen the light of day in New York City.

Mark was in love with this Jay woman. He admitted as much later on. He was still working with her when we got back to New York. She was all for injecting shock into the play, making the character ribald, even offensive, and Mark shared that desire. On the other hand, I took a surgeon's view of the script, scrupulously mining it for anything that didn't ring true, anything that sounded the least like braggadocio. Mark and I had a tussle over a line he invented that I thought didn't sound like her: "As Joan Crawford once said, 'If you want the girl next door, go next door.'" He won that fight and it is often quoted as one of the more memorable lines from the show. What bothered the hell out of me about Jay Allen was that she didn't give a damn about being true to Vreeland's character.

I once thought Mark and I were as close as any married couple. Our relationship was one of the most intimate I have ever had. I didn't have a mate and he did, so naturally he had a bifurcated fealty. Still, his continuing to work with Jay absolutely crushed me. I told him our contract forbade him to work on the play with another writer. He said, "I don't agree," and when he said that, a surge from the bottom of my gut rose up, a tsunami of rage stored from years back, and I let him have it. I said a lot of things, I felt so betrayed, but the words didn't matter, it was the power of the onslaught. Mark told me later that even in the teeth of it, he was thinking, "Boy! If she could ever do that on stage . . ."

Back in New York, a couple of months after San Diego, I got a call from Jay. She chirped, "Well, I've rewritten your script, and it only took me two hours." My mumbled retort: "And it only took me six years."

"Well, darling," she said. "You're not a writer."

I prayed, I really prayed, that I would love the script, but reading it was like being slapped in the face with a wet flounder. The most infuriating thing was her careless insertion of anachronistic clichés. Vreeland never resorted to clichés. She *coined* clichés.

I called Jay's agent as instructed, and told him I wasn't interested.

I didn't think Mark should be reimbursed for his living expenses in San Diego since he spent his time out there working against me. William Morris withheld the money, and Mark's lawyer threatened a suit. This just as we were on the verge of making a deal with the Manhattan Theater Club in New York. Mark refused to sign unless he was paid.

As far as I understood it, he was suing me. I sensed vindictiveness. I was still smarting from being billed by him and his mate Michael Sharp for the huge amount they lavished on the set in Sag Harbor without consulting me. I was the Money Bags for this show.

As long as this was happening, there would be no contract with the Manhattan Theater Club. I appealed to our agent, Gil. He shrugged helplessly. There would be no assistance coming from William Morris. I was in agony. Months went by. I was finally obliged to pay up so that we could proceed with negotiations, but I couldn't bear to have anything to do with Mark for a long time after that.

Momentum

*A*FTER EACH PERFORMANCE IN THE PAST, NO MATTER HOW POSI-tive the response had been, we seemed to fall back into the void; exactly where we had been before. Now, starting with the performance at the nightclub McGraw's, it was like a slow-moving freight train. There were stoppages, longueurs, gaps along the way, but things lurched inexorably forward. Interest in the play and Vreeland had developed a momentum of its own: the Allen and O'Brien meetings that spring and summer leading to the run at the Old Globe in December, then to the Manhattan Theater Club the following September.

I started taking tango lessons. Vreeland adored dancing, she wanted to be a dancer, and I wanted to perform at least a couple of tango moves in the play. This was dangerous, it was difficult to trust that I wouldn't look ridiculous. It had to be beautifully executed. My partner was a young woman. After six weeks with her leading me around, I could manage to let myself go with the hip sway, the sinuous glide for whole moments at a time. I discovered an exciting Astor Piazzolla tango that had the necessary *oomph* to launch me into it.

I also wanted to illustrate dance steps from *The Dying Swan*. I went to the Lincoln Center Library and studied Pavlova dying, swooping her arms over and down, and bending her torso over one extended leg. I tried it out on the porch one day in front of my buddy Carol Morley. She didn't laugh.

Other things happened in this period. While I was in San Diego an Argentinian woman I let stay in my apartment painted the whole place in lurid pinks and purples. Quite a feat considering the 25-foot ceilings. I told her I hated it and fled upstate. She repainted it all white again. She was fast but she was furious. I kicked her out and found out later she had informed the rent control authorities that I owned another residence. Meanwhile a group of young filmmakers asked if they could rent the apartment for two weeks for $5,000. Not knowing if we were going to get the play on at all, I accepted and went back up to my house. The two weeks turned into three and still going—they built a kitchen in my living room—and MTC was now happening, so I had to move to a hotel with 22-year-old City Kitty who was on a hydration regimen requiring needles, an IV stand and several plastic bags of fluid.

We opened at the Manhattan Theater Club in September of 1995. The MTC audience is infamous for resembling the living dead. Even the management jokes about it. The first preview audience literally screamed at every line; this had happened to me before, I supposed these were extreme fans. But after that, the regular subscribers sat there like Easter Island heads.

The Manhattan Theater Club stage was an open square with seats on three sides, once again lessening the effect of direct address. I just decided to ignore the seats on the sides. A few feet separated the acting space from the first row, which was on the same level and highly visible in the light spill; there were times when I found myself inadvertently locking eyes with individuals in workout suits with shopping bags, or friends, or Al Hirschfeld. Disconcerting to say the least.

Nicky told me he had hired the perfect stage manager for me. "Divas love him. He's great at massaging feet!" The idea that Nicky saw me as a diva was perplexing. The man was very sweet, but entirely unequipped to call intercom, doorbell, and phone cues, which were so bloody important and they were coming in consistently late or not at all, and driving me insane.

Various luminaries came backstage. Kenneth, the premier hair-dresser of the eighties, a big, dashing man who recalled dyeing and re-dyeing Vreeland's hair as she kept complaining, "Not black enough!" Richard Avedon came back—boyish looking, tousled white hair—and demonstrated for me her exaggerated posture. When he first came to work for her, she called him "Aberdeen."

Ali MacGraw came back, she had been an assistant under Vreeland before her film career. She told me how terrifying she was. Assistants were called "Miss," as in, "Miss! Hand me that photograph."

I was not blind to Mrs. Vreeland's downside. There were people who loathed her, and probably with good reason, but I couldn't go there. People asked me if I had ever met her; I didn't want to, I think she would have been supremely uninterested in me.

My old pal George Furth showed up. He called to me over the heads of the backstage crowd: "You don't have an ending, you know!" This infuriated me, as usual. As usual, he was right. We didn't have an ending for the play.

A year passed between the end of the run at the Manhattan Theater Club and the play opening at the Westside Theater, but it was hardly a dull one. I went up the Amazon with Patricia Neal. I replaced the vacationing Parthy in *Show Boat* on Broadway for a month. I won a Drama Desk Award and an Obie. The *New Yorker* magazine called, they wanted to photograph me as Vreeland. I panicked. Once again, Bettie O. came to my rescue, fixing my wig, running out to buy false fingernails, gluing them on and painting them red—all in about fifteen minutes. *Women's Wear Daily* also photographed me in costume. Finally, and not incidentally, I was evicted from my apartment of thirty-seven years and I had to put down my beloved twenty-three-year-old City Kitty, aka Sydney.

There were meetings with the producers Fran and Barry Weissler, their protégé David Stone, and Amy Nederlander to produce the play. Nothing was certain. There were tenants in the Westside at the time, we had to wait.

Somewhere in here, Mark and I went together to see a woman therapist he knew. Whatever took place in there, the anger dissolved itself into a dew. This was the first time I realized how different his goals were from mine. I wanted to reestablish my acting chops and also to create a little gem of a play. He wanted a commercial hit. He once remarked that I thought "hit" was a dirty word. Nothing wrong with wanting a big success, why else would he devote so much effort if it wasn't to aim for fame and money? At least in the end the play established his credentials as a writer.

The Inevitable Ending

*U*P TO THIS POINT, WE HAD FOUGHT THE NOTION OF A BIOGRAPHical play. As we demonstrated in the Bay Street production, neither of us was interested in a happy, or any kind of conventional ending. Ironically, we kept finding out that for the play to work, in order to create belief in the character, we needed as many details of conventional life as we could pack in.

The truth of what had happened to Mrs. Vreeland after she was fired seemed almost too perfect, too much like a fairy-tale ending. I was told the Metropolitan Museum had reluctantly hired her. Friends in high places like Bill Blass and Jackie Kennedy persuaded them to do so. They wanted her to at least have a sinecure, her name on a door. Nobody predicted what was actually going to happen. I couldn't imagine how I could relay this information without resorting to lengthy tracts of exposition. I disliked the idea of the audience needing to have prior knowledge to appreciate it.

I started with the idea of Vreeland trying to avoid a phone call from a curator at the Met: he wants to talk to her about a job there. She mutters, "Why is everybody trying to put me in a museum?" I thought of the times I had been out of work and dying for a job when an offer would come—a lead role in a play, it would be a six-month run in Alaska. I was walking along a stretch of road upstate I had been walking for the past five years, addressing the trees in Vreelandese, when the words flew into my head: "I don't care if they've got the Shroud of Turin in there! I am not interested." I didn't have the faintest notion what the Shroud of Turin was; I must have been channeling Vreeland, but it struck me as the perfect expression of her repugnance for the job.

Finally we had a satisfying ending: the lights going down on her vigorously refusing the job on the phone, while describing at length what she would do if she took it.

The day I walked into the Westside Theater and saw the set, I nearly wept. The house was a perfect size, 250 seats and at last we had a proscenium. The designer, Jim Noone, had created a perfect replica of the Garden in Hell. Real flowers couldn't have competed with the gorgeous silk peonies, parrot tulips, Madonna lilies, and quince branches I was given.

The Chair

*A*S VREELAND, I WANTED TO PUT HER HANDS ON SOMETHING; there's something fascinating to me about the way people in the fashion world handle fabrics so authoritatively. So we wrote into the script a chair with a slipcover that's not quite to her liking. Once or twice she goes over to it and gives it a tug. Then at some point she picks up the *Post* to read the rest of the article that Mark wrote:

> *While the . . . oracle of beauty serenely traipsed Europe with her seventeen pieces of Vuitton luggage, friends back home have been frantically rallying to find her a job. Any job. The down-at-heels doyenne with the cigar-store Indian looks seemed as enduring as fashion itself: What went wrong? No one appears to know the exact cause of her abrupt dumping. Was it the plummeting ad revenues? The takeout from Lutèce? Or was it that, according to an undisclosed source at the magazine, "her era was over"?*

She puts the *Post* down, looks the chair, goes over to it and rips the slipcover off and throws it on the floor. Later in the play, she picks the slipcover up and, while talking, gathers it up and places it in the chair like a pillow.

The slipcover that Michael Sharp made in Sag Harbor was a light-weight flowered chintz that flew off with one tug, and when gathered into a ball it transformed itself into a pillow with a flower magically placed dead center.

I could not seem to get Nicky to recognize the chair's importance. At the Westside, the cover was a bulky upholstery fabric that wouldn't slide off or bundle up easily, and the chair itself was placed like a lonely relative in an upstage corner, well out of my line of vision. I couldn't risk arguing the point with him, I was afraid he would blow up. I had already experienced this in San Diego the day he arrived a half-hour late for rehearsal and found that I had gone ahead and started with the stage manager. He must have seen it as a threat to his authority. The slightest objection could turn his charm into vitriolic screaming.

Finally

ASIDE FROM THE CHAIR, WE FINALLY HAD WHAT MARK AND I wanted: preshow music, Mabel Mercer singing "From This Moment On" with no joy-killing interruptions, and an intermission. For Françoise, the maid on the intercom, we had the beautiful voice and impeccable accent of Jacqueline Chambord, the head of the Alliance Française. My costume—simple black trousers, black cashmere sweater, and low-heeled black pumps custom-made but nonetheless agonizing— was put together by Michael Krass. I already had the jewelry: the tusk necklace and a pair of heavy bone bracelets I had found in a Turkish shop in the Village. David Segal was responsible for the lighting; and I had Ira Mont, the prince of stage managers, thoroughly professional, a meticulous bell ringer and door buzzer. I could have been lonely backstage, but I managed to persuade Bettie O. to be my aide-de-camp in the dressing room. Along with the box-office guys and the house manager, we were one happy little family.

It occurred to me that the last time I did something like this was the *Arsenic and Old Lace* performance for my school's PTA. It was okay for me to be the star when I was the only one onstage. It was the only possible way. Although, at one point in this journey, I remember Mark complaining that I was "playing Vreeland like a supporting player." Old habits die hard.

We opened on a Tuesday. I had made it a rule a long time ago to never read reviews after an opening but this time I was told to take a peek at the *Times* the following Sunday and there was a half-page photograph of me as Vreeland with a lovely review below it. There may have been some caveats—I heard that the *Times*' Ben Brantley's review of the Manhattan Theater Club show had not been great, so the producers wouldn't let him come back to rereview it—but it just didn't matter. The houses were packed. It was a hit, a palpable hit.

Suddenly there were publicity events, fashion-show appearances, book signings—*D.V.* was republished with an introduction written by me. I was suddenly an authority on acting, asked to give drama-school graduation addresses. I didn't enjoy these occasions. What could I tell them? "Don't do it"?

The dressing room at the Westside was a narrow space and people who wanted to see me after the show were asked to wait in the house. Every night, I came out to meet the most surprising array of notables: Esther Williams ("I'm a bathing-suit designer now!"), Debbie Reynolds, Douglas Fairbanks Jr., Bulgari of Bulgari Jewelry, Princess Marella Agnelli, Grace Mirabella (who replaced Vreeland at *Vogue*), as well as theater people like Eileen Atkins, Elaine Stritch, Ben Gazzara, Lauren Bacall ("I knew her, you know."). I was quite abashed to see Arthur Laurents and Stephen Sondheim waiting to see me. And then there were the people who had worked with Vreeland and loved her, talking to me about her with tears in their eyes. The only person who insisted on coming backstage was Bea Arthur, who crashed into the dressing room bellowing, "Mary Lou-EEESE!" and knocked Bettie O. into the coat hangers on the wall.

One night when I mentioned Edwina d'Erlanger, a society name from a former era, a gaunt old couple in ancient finery sitting in the second row murmured reverently, "Oh! Edwina!" Another night as I made my entrance, I heard Carol Channing growl, "Di-anna!"

And then there was the Vreeland family. I was very glad they were pleased with the play. Freckie and his wife came from Morocco, and took me to the 21 Club after the show. Mrs. Vreeland's older son, Tim, sent me a long, loving, handwritten letter from California. Alexander reappeared, apparently satisfied this time. He brought his tow-headed children to the show, who scrambled onto the set afterwards, exclaiming over the familiar objects of their great grandmother's living room. Finally there was Nicky, Diana's other beloved grandson who had become a monk. He arrived in his saffron robes with a scarf for me from the Dalai Lama. He looked at me with tears in his eyes: "Did you love my grand-mother?" I said I did, I did. I still do.

We ran for eleven months. It took a year for my feet to recover. Having worked for such a long time on Mrs. Vreeland's stories, her voice and mannerisms, she was deeply embedded in me, and there were times onstage when I had the sensation of being out of my body, float-ing above the lines; I felt the audience breathing with me. Actors rarely get the chance to inhabit a role this long, which is too bad. I feel ex-tremely lucky to have had it.

I couldn't have done this play until most of my family was dead. I could not have withstood their lack of encouragement. Taffy was still alive, but after confronting her, the articles about actors in mental in-stitutions finally stopped coming; she sent flowers instead.

My family believed in cremation. After the deaths of my mother, father, and brother, stones bearing their names and dates were placed in the family plot in the cemetery in Sherman, Connecticut. When we laid the stone for my brother, I took the opportunity as the last of the line to lay one for myself. The stone is carved with my name, date of birth, and the words: "She's the best thing in it."

After *Full Gallop*

*T*HINGS DEFINITELY CHANGED. THE ROLES GOT A LOT BETTER. I was cast as the blind, cancer-ridden mother in John Guare's *Bosoms and Neglect* at New York's Signature Theater. It was one of the best roles I've ever had, right up my alley. The second act of the play is one long battle between me in my hospital bed and my son. I was lying in the bed in the rehearsal hall one day when Guare came up to me and said, "You know, you're not really in bed." This mysterious remark was the best direction I could have gotten: she may have been dying, but she had the force of a blast furnace.

I got the part of Fräulein Schneider in the Roundabout Theater's 1998 revival of *Cabaret*. I wanted it—it was the perfect follow-up to *Full Gallop*. But it turned out to be a bitch of a role to play. Originally written for Lotte Lenya, the queen of Weimar Germany, both of her songs "So What?" and "What Would You Do?" were humorless dirges. The German accent was another bugaboo. To sing, "So vat? Hoo cahrs," and "Vat vud yoo doo?" over and over wasn't easy, let me tell you. On the other hand, this was the first time I played a woman who is kissed by a man.

I thought the director, Sam Mendes, was terrific. I liked him and I think he liked me, but he made my life hell. Instead of giving encouragement, he kept reinforcing my doubts about my ability. He made me sit face-to-face with him and sing my song while he interrupted with comments like, "No self pity!" and "Don't be maudlin!" Of course the last thing I wanted was to be maudlin, but this is no way to get a performance out of an actor.

Another time the composer, John Kander, whom I had known

since *Flora the Red Menace*, took me into a room to coach me. John is a very dear man, a friend, but his special coaching only made me more certain I was not coming up to the mark. I simply needed time to develop the material.

An actor can bulge to huge proportions and then in less time than it takes to cough they can shrivel to a speck of dust. We're like fever dreams. After our first run-through in the rehearsal hall, Sam gave notes, and in front of everybody he said to me, "I didn't see anything going on in your eyes." I asked him afterwards if could he please take me aside to give notes. He quickly apologized; he knew he shouldn't have done it, but I think in some strange way he enjoyed embarrassing me.

The great thing about Sam was that he knew exactly what he wanted. Our entrances and exits were precisely timed. The show moved like a smooth machine. He spent a great deal of time on the sound, getting it right. The interior of the Henry Miller Theater on West 43rd was gutted and fitted out with tables and chairs. Sam had a tussle with *Playbill* magazine over not wanting them given out at the start because this interfered with the audience's illusion of being in an actual cabaret.

During tech rehearsals the curtain bows were practiced. I noticed that each lead was given a single bow except for Ron Rifkin who played Herr Schultz and myself; we came out together. During a break I went up to Sam and asked why we couldn't have separate bows. He said Ron was afraid that if he came out after me the applause might drop. I was stunned. I didn't usually give a crap about bows, but this wasn't right. "Then why doesn't he come out before me?" Oh no, oh no, the bigger the billing, the later the bowing. That's the rule. Though I believe our billing was of equal size. I grumbled some more and Sam said, "Oh, Mary Louise, don't be so petty! Bows don't mean anything." I looked him in the eye: "You know as well as I do, it's all about perception." He sighed. I stared at him. Finally he said he would speak to him. But he didn't, and I couldn't bring myself to make a stink.

It's interesting to note that the *Times* gave *Cabaret* a lukewarm review, because from the first preview on it was a huge success. Celebrities swarmed to it. Every night after the show when I opened my dressing room door, all of them seemed to be standing there: Billy Crystal, Kirk Douglas, Tom Waits, Emma Thompson, blah blah blah.

The dressing rooms were old-fashioned, two to a floor, with the chorus at the top, five flights up. Across the hall on my floor were John Benjamin Hickey and Denis O'Hare. John is irresistible, the most sociable of creatures. I had a terrific crush on Denis, something about his perfect teeth. His lack of ego playing a clarinet in the band while playing a featured role, his passion for poetry and art, as well as his brilliance as an actor makes him a truly rare bird. Ron Rifkin and I seated backstage right waiting for our cue, would watch Denis stage left perform brilliant little pantomimes with his hat, newspaper and briefcase, never acknowledging his audience or our pantomimed applause. The backstage precision of quick changes was wonderful to watch. I can still see the row of pre-rolled pink stockings for the Kit Kat Girls lined up along the back of one set. The backstage crew knew how tough "Vut Vud Yoo Do?" was. When I came off after the song, they greeted me with silent applause. One night they were holding up signs with "7s" on them, like figure-skating judges.

Alan Cumming was adorable. We went to tea together one day and, leaning over the steaming pot, he murmured in his lovely Scottish burr, "Mary Louise, would you care for some Ecstasy?" He was living life like a cabaret. There were some pretty naughty goings-on in that theater after-hours.

About three months into the run, the Condé Nast building under construction next door collapsed and fell onto the theater, along with other buildings. The show was shut down until they could move it into Studio 54. I left at this point to do *Full Gallop* in London.

1999: *Full Gallop* in London

I PLAYED THE HAMPSTEAD THEATER. THE PRODUCTION WAS NOT the success it had been. The Hampstead audience seemed generally mystified. I think the Hampstead's relationship to London is rather like that of the New Jersey Rep to Manhattan. I don't think Londoners ordinarily make the trip out there to see a play.

I read the reviews years later and was surprised to see they were pretty good. But there was no publicity. Every night when I came out to go home, the lobby would be empty. One of the few moments I recall with pleasure was coming out to find the actor Jonathan Pryce waiting to see me. That was a thrill.

One unexpected benefit from our labors has been the demand for *Full Gallop* in countries all over the world. It's a perfect vehicle for older actresses not only in the U.S., but South America, Sweden, France, Germany, Denmark, and Italy, and some sixteen years later it's still going. The latest production was done last year in Paris.

2006: *Grey Gardens*

W HEN I GOT A CALL ABOUT A MUSICAL BASED ON *GREY GARDENS*, that depressing film about those two pathetic old bags in their filthy house with cat piss everywhere, I thought, Oh boy, good luck with that. But I wasn't asked to audition and it was only a workshop, and this was December and the workshop was in Florida, so I said yes. The role was Big Edie. Christine Ebersole was going to play Little Edie. The show's composer, Scott Frankel, had requested us for the roles. How often does that happen in an actor's life?

The first time I saw Christine, on the plane down to Florida, I was too intimidated to say hello. Once, years ago, when we were both in a one-day backers' audition, she caught me borrowing her curling iron backstage and I thought she was going to slug me. But she didn't seem to remember, and we got along fine. As things turned out, we didn't see a lot of each other, because most of the time in Florida was spent working on the first act, with her playing Little Edie. Big Edie didn't appear until the second act, so I stood around a lot. Scott told me he was writing a song for me called "Jerry Likes My Corn." He played it for me. I loved it. But I was grumpy, as usual, feeling neglected. The one great treat was playing running charades with the cast and crew in the big main living room, a game that apparently started in Hollywood with film actors—funny ones like Mike Myers and Julie Kavner, who, to escape rabid fans in public places, rented a hotel ballroom to play.

There were more workshops over the next year, and I was always available. I still didn't see what I was being given here. In my usual way, I was waiting for the letdown, looking at the whole project with a huge stick up my rear. At the same time, I was watching the *Grey Gardens* DVD over and over, getting Edith Beale in my head and under my skin, rolling her words around on my tongue.

Michael Greif, the director, was very tolerant. I had a hard time with the song lyrics, especially since I was now at an age where nothing came easily to mind. He seemed to trust me, and that gave me permission to flourish. Michael is a complex individual. I wish I knew him better, could sit down and have long conversations with him about life in general.

I loved all these guys, for themselves as well as their talent: Scott Frankel; Michael Korie, who wrote the lyrics; and Doug Wright, who wrote the wonderful book; and Paul Huntley, who, of course, made me a gorgeous wig of long white hair.

For the whole second act I was onstage in bed. I sang in bed. My voice never felt so full and easy. I don't know why that should have been. When words occasionally deserted me, Christine bailed me out. Except once, when she couldn't, because it was the last line of the show; in previews we were trying out different show endings, and I had the line, "Well, you still have your dancing" as the light fades to black. One night, as she told me later, I apparently said, "Well, you still have your tennis." There's no tennis in *Grey Gardens*. As for Christine Ebersole, I loved her, too, still do, with all my heart. Working with her was an unexpected bonus. We were a team.

More George

GEORGE FURTH POPPED UP IN MY LIFE ON A REGULAR BASIS OVER the years. He would call from L.A. to tell me how to change my life, how so and so had been living in her car and wrote a book about it and was now on all the talk shows, and once in the Seventies we went to Europe together with his script for what would be become Kander and Ebb's musical *The Act* starring Liza Minnelli. He asked if the writing was keeping me up (no computers or tablets in those days, just paper and pencil) and I told him no, only the erasing. There was a good deal of erasing. And then the hotel maid in Paris accidentally threw the script out. He was a Christian Scientist so he worked through this calamity.

George was a compulsive gossip. He would never allow himself to be interviewed or appear on a talk show because he knew he'd be sued by somebody. He drove me mad repeating things I had said to perfect strangers. But in the last few years he would call to tell me funny jokes. He seemed to me to have mellowed. We started talking about taking trip to Mexico together. I knew in my heart it was probably not a good idea but I put off telling him. He said he had a cold that wouldn't quit and he was going to San Francisco for the weekend, and a couple of days later I heard he had died of a heart attack. I felt a large wedge of my life fall away.

*I*T STRIKES ME THAT I WOULD NOT HAVE SUCCEEDED IN THIS BUSI-
ness without the gay men in my life. I would have been up a creek
without their encouragement and their sensibility. Most straight men
reacted poorly to my clowning. They didn't get me, but the men I knew
and worked with did, they gave me my career.

The Obies

*W*HILE WE WERE STILL AT PLAYWRIGHTS, I GOT AN INVITATION
to the Obie Awards. When I got an Obie in 1995 for *Full Gallop*,
the evening was very Village, anarchic and fun. I recall Uta Hagen
mounting the stage to receive a lifetime achievement award. She was
wearing a hat. She stepped up to the podium and said, "Excuse the hat,
my hair looks like ka-ka today."

The 2005-2006 Obies were presented at NYU's Skirball Center.
I wore a dressy dress and little backless pumps, and took a cab across
town. In the lobby people were milling around; I spotted Christine
standing with Scott and Michael and Doug and joined them. The
awards began, we went in, took our seats. A lifetime award was given
to the actor Reed Birney. I was astonished; I had worked with Reed
years before, he was so talented, and I had wondered ever since what
became of him. Obviously he had been having a great career I knew
nothing about. Then Michael Feingold got up and read a list of actors
who had died that year. He left out Maureen Stapleton, a rather large
omission, and I almost yelled out her name. I didn't. The usually loose
occasion had become formal. Then, Christine got up to get her Obie.
The awards went on and my face and arms began to burn as it dawned
on me that I wasn't going to get one. How could I have imagined, just
because I got an invitation . . . but it was because I got the invitation
that I thought . . .

The awards ended. I saw Christine, Scott, and the others, and somehow I thought I would join them upstairs. I waited as people filed past toward the doors, but when they didn't appear after a while, I couldn't stand there any longer. I walked back toward my apartment. I saw the window of a coffee house on the corner of Waverly Place, still open, only two others in it. It looked like a Hopper painting. I went in, sat at the window with a cup of coffee, marveling that I had walked all the way from Washington Square back to Seventh Avenue in those stupid little backless pumps.

Grey Gardens went to Broadway with an army of producers. The main money one was a wildly wealthy couple who lavished expensive gifts on the cast members—genuine cowhide satchels that required a forklift to get onto your shoulder with only a banana inside, humungous triple-thick terry robes, and floral displays worthy of the Tomb of the Unknown Soldier—but at the same time they seemed amazingly short-sighted in their dealings with us. Christine once referred to their representative as "dumb as a box of hair."

There were two little girls in the show, so they had what is called on Broadway a "wrangler" to look after them. This rather large woman took up permanent residence on the stairs outside my dressing room door and reported to the producers every wild joke I made at their expense. They were very upset when my dresser, Vangeli Kaseluris, gathered up a bunch of different-colored Crocs that had been given to everyone in the cast and sold them on eBay. A long-standing custom on Broadway opening nights is for the producer to give every company member a show memento. These days, what with the slew of producers required to produce a show, it's possible in a single night to acquire a truckload of Tiffany key rings, ashtrays, picture frames, diaries, hats, jackets, and mugs, mugs, mugs, all embossed with the show's name. I don't have a special memorabilia cabinet in my rec room, so what to do with them? I don't need coffee mugs, I don't really want to wear advertisements on my back, and I could use the silver picture frame, but not with *"Godspell, 1985"* engraved on it. For these same reasons I can't pass them along as gifts, so I end up shoving them in closets. Now, happily, it's becoming the custom in many shows to sell them on eBay. They make dandy souvenirs.

Except for a few minutes at the top of the first act, I was offstage while everybody else was on. I would have been very lonely if it hadn't been for the sweet, young, sensitive and funny Vangeli, who dressed me. As different as we were he and I connected. Van was invaluable as a stylist, helping me choose gowns for important occasions and then making it possible to return them the next day. I objected that I was too old to wear this gorgeous red chiffon gown he borrowed for opening night, but it worked, I looked pretty fabulous.

In 2007, Christine and I were both nominated for Tony Awards—her for Leading Actress in a Musical, me for Featured Actress. Van and I shopped for hours looking for a gown. We finally chose something very simple, black, with a neckline that ran across the collarbone. We brought it to the dressing room and invited Christine up to have a look at it. She was shocked, and adamant: "Oh no, you can't wear that!" She said it looked like something you would wear to a cocktail party, not to a major event. It wasn't nearly formal enough. But Van and I stuck to it. I wanted to look understated. Elegant. To quote Mrs. Vreeland, "Elegance is refusal."

The Tonys

*T*HERE IS NO DESCRIBING THE AGONIES THAT GO ALONG WITH these events. Leading up to the Big Night, there are endless functions that a nominee is expected to attend. I recall, at one of these in the upstairs Sardi's room, seeing Jane Alexander stump glumly through the crowd wearing what looked like an ordinary cotton dress; she must have gone through this so many times.

The Tonys are supposedly given by actors to their peers. I'm often surprised to learn who the Tony voters are, and wonder how they came to be chosen. The actual Tony presenters are television and film actors. Bleachers are set up across the street from the theater for the Great Unwashed to watch and scream when they spot a television star. There is a paparazzi room you must pass through, just like they do in Hollywood, for cameras that are really waiting for the television and film stars to come through.

For a nominee, the evening is one long slog. Once you're in your seat, it's rare to spot fellow sufferers in the crowd; the audience appears to be entirely made up of marketing people. Sitting there on the night I won, I joked that if I didn't win I was going to get up, give the camera the finger, and march back up the aisle. I was able to invent a scenario for losing, but apparently not one for winning. I couldn't prepare a speech "just in case." Of course I wanted to win, I had been nominated for a Tony in *Cabaret*. There's nothing more painful than being nominated and not winning.

This night, when my name was called, I went numb. I walked up there and Donny Osmond, of all people, handed me the Tony, kissed me on the cheek, and stepped aside. I looked at the audience. I was completely blank. Into my head popped this hound dog I knew that could howl "Happy Birthday." I howled. I mumbled something about wondering if I ever won would I feel like a fraud, and then added that I didn't. As if I'd said the wittiest thing in the world, wild applause. Then I was hustled through an interminable gamut of paparazzi cameras flashing—I had no idea there were so many news outlets. "Look over here, Mary Louise!" "Look this way!" "Look here!" "Look up!" "Look down!" My feet were killing me. The first moment I experienced real pleasure was in the grocery store the next day, when I saw my picture on the front page of *The New York Times*.

Winning a Tony is often followed by a longish period of unemployment, and I had some lengthy interludes between calls. I thought

I should be going up for bigger roles on television, but it occurred to me that if I wanted them my neck needed to see a plastic surgeon.

The doctor's multimillion-dollar outer office sporting mammoth Steuben sculptures filled me with resentment, and when he told me that I would require a 24-hour nurse, would not be able to eat solids or speak for a week, and that I would have to sign a paper relieving them of all responsibility if I died on the table, I opted for scarves. It was the not speaking for a week that did it.

I was on crutches from a fractured pelvis when I got the call to read for a play at Lincoln Center. I was afraid they might think I wasn't up for the gig. A friend suggested I tell them I fell off my horse, to which John Seidman added, "You fell off your high horse." I had done a reading of the play. The play was *4000 Miles* by Amy Herzog. The role was an old time lefty grandmother who is visited by her grandson. I really wanted this part.

I may have been on crutches, but this time it wasn't from shooting myself in the foot. This experience was the most fulfilling I've ever had in the theater. It's a beautifully written script, skillfully directed by Daniel Aukin. Lincoln Center's André Bishop and Bernie Gersten were wonderful to us. And the three other actors in the play, Greta Lee, Zoe Winters, and Gabriel Ebert—all in their twenties, all fine actors—were gifts from heaven. I treasure their friendship to this day.

Nowadays

*F*INDING MYSELF GETTING HAPPIER AND HAPPIER THE LONGER I'M away from having to put my face on tape—having to look good, or look any way at all, I finally reach a point of believing with all my heart that I have no taste for it anymore; no wish to be wandering around in the broiling heat or the snows of Kilimanjaro, in Chinatown or Upper Montclair, looking for a casting office; no desire to perform in anything eight exhausting times a week, then the phone rings: "They want you to read for—" and this snake leaps out of my mouth: "What time?" The need to perform doesn't die. It's like lust; it's like throwing a lit match on a pile of dry hay.

Nowadays I'm up mostly for old lady roles. It's surprising how many of those there are. My one rule is: it has to be an old lady who robs a bank or smokes pot or something. No Alzheimer's roles, thank you very much. Unless she's funny.

The last details of any story are never satisfactory.
—D.V.

I DIDN'T INTEND TO WRITE THIS BOOK. I STARTED OUT TO WRITE about the eight-year journey of getting *Full Gallop* to the stage. A sort of primer for people who wanted to do their own one person shows. Naturally I had to include background, how I came to write the play and so on, as circumspect and amusing as I could make it, because my life wasn't the main topic. Halfway through I showed what I had written to a few close friends, each of whom shortly returned it with glazed eyes and polite murmurs. I was shocked by their reticence. I grabbed their lapels and demanded to know what they thought. "You aren't in it!" they yelped. "We want to know about you!" "This doesn't sound like you." I didn't get it. I couldn't make this about me, I'm not well known, I didn't have a glittering career studded with affairs and celebrities. Besides, I didn't want to write about me, whoever that was. I never want to be me, that's why I'm only happy when I'm playing other people! I was also terrified of anything that wasn't funny or ironic because that was my stock in trade. Everything in my life was up for laughs. Nevertheless, I tried to get more honest, and the deeper I dug the more unfunny things got. I kept bumping into embarrassing incidents, inexplicable behaviors that I didn't want to look at. It came to me that after fifty years I was still carrying around this load of resentment, shame and guilt. I was having a terrible time. I quit writing more than once, the process was just too painful. Finally, after a great deal of writing, rewriting and hating every minute of it, I began to see things more clearly. I had revelation after revelation. I saw I had been the villain in my own story. And to my amazement once I realized this the anger and guilt, the whole load, lifted. Flew out the window. Freedom! I never enjoyed life so much as I do today.

I like to think of myself as a proud member of the Character Actors' Club whose names may not be familiar to the general public. Their faces may be familiar from television appearances, but not their names. Their names and their work in play after play are well known in the theater world. A few of these wonderful performers I've worked with or have seen over the years include Marylouise Burke, Jonathan Hadary, Byron Jennings, Lisa Emory, David Pittu, Reed Birney, Kristine Nielson, Mark Blum, Peter Friedman, Laila Robbins, Lewis J. Stadlin, Linda Emond, Mark-Linn Baker, Joan MacIntosh, Michael McGrath, Susan Blommaert, Henry Stram, Carol Morley, Christine Ebersole, Tom Lacy, Mark Harelik, Denny Dillon, McIntyre Dixon, John Seidman, Mary Testa, David Aaron Baker, Mark Chmiel, John Christopher Jones, Denis O'Hare, John Glover, Brian Murray, John Benjamin Hickey, Dick Lattessa, Julie Halston, Polly Holliday, Martin Moran, Harriet Harris, Maria Tucci, Michael Potts, Kate Skinner, Deborah Rush and Patricia Connolly. These are only a few. I hope no one is offended by being, or not being, listed here.

WHO'S WHO

ABBOTT, GEORGE – Broadway playwright, director, actor, producer. *Jumbo, Pal Joey, High Button Shoes, Where's Charley, Call Me Madam, Wonderful Town, Pajama Game, On Your Toes, Damn Yankees, Fiorello!,* and *A Funny Thing Happened on the Way to the Forum*. Directed his final production at age 102.

ADRIAN – American costume designer for MGM films of the 30s and 40s. Creator of the ruby slippers for *The Wizard of Oz*.

AGNELLI, PRINCESS MARELLA – wife of Fiat industrialist, Gianni Agnelli and designer, created a series of houses and gardens spread throughout Turin, Rome, Milan, New York, St. Moritz, and Marrakesh.

ALEXANDER, JANE – award-winning stage and film actress (*The Great White Hope, The Sisters Rosensweig*) former director of the National Endowment for the Arts.

ALEXANDRE – hairdresser to the stars, created Elizabeth Taylor's coiffure for *Cleopatra*.

ALLEN, JAY PRESSON – adapter of novels for plays and movies: Films, *The Prime of Miss Jean Brodie* and *Travels with My Aunt*. Wrote and directed the play *Tru*.

ALLEN, LEWIS – theater and film producer. Among his productions, the Broadway musical, *Annie* and the films, *Fahrenheit 451* and *Lord of the Flies*.

ALLEN, WOODY – filmmaker, *Annie Hall, Hannah and Her Sisters, Manhattan*.

ARDEN, EVE – film actress, Joan Crawford's sidekick in *Mildred Pierce*.

ARKIN, ALAN – actor, director, composer. Stage, *Luv, Enter Laughing* (Tony). Directed *Little Murders, The Sunshine Boys*. Film, *Catch-22, The Heart is a Lonely Hunter, Little Miss Sunshine* (Oscar), *Argo*. Wrote Harry Belafonte hit *Banana Boat*.

ARMSTRONG, LOUIS – jazz legend, trumpeter and singer. First African-American jazz musician to cross over into popular music.

ARNAZ, LUCIE – actress (*They're Playing Our Song*) and producer (*Lucy and Desi: A Home Movie*.)

ARTHUR, BEATRICE – star of TV series, *Maude* and *The Golden Girls*. Played Vera Charles opposite Angela Lansbury in the musical, *Mame*.

ARTHUR, JEAN – actress in Frank Capra classics, *Mr. Deeds Goes to Town, You Can't Take It With You, Mr. Smith Goes to Washington*.

ATKINS, EILEEN – British actress, writer, co-creator with Jean Marsh of *Upstairs, Downstairs*. Films include *Gosford Park*.

AUKIN, DANIEL – directed critically acclaimed plays, *4000 Miles, Bad Jews*.

AVEDON, RICHARD – fashion and portrait photographer. Wide range of his work contributed to the acceptance of photography as an art form.

AZENBERG, EMANUEL "MANNY" – theater producer and general manager whose professional relationship with playwright Neil Simon spans thirty-three years.

BACALL, LAUREN – Hollywood star of the golden age and later Broadway musicals.

BACHARACH, BURT – composer of 73 top 40 hits.

BAGNOLD, ENID – British author of plays, *The Chalk Garden*, *A Matter of Gravity* and novel, *National Velvet*.

BAKER, JAMES – former U.S. Secretary of State under George H.W. Bush, Secretary of Treasury and Chief of Staff under Ronald Reagan.

BALLARD, KAYE – musical theater and cabaret star. Originated the role of Rosalie in *Carnival*.

BANKHEAD, TALLULAH – star of Broadway's golden age, originated the role of Sabina in Thornton Wilder's *The Skin of Our Teeth*.

BARER, MARSHALL – book writer and lyricist for *Once Upon a Mattress*.

BARRYMORE, JOHN – Hollywood star, *Grand Hotel*, *Twentieth Century*, *Midnight*, *A Bill of Divorcement*, *Dinner at Eight*.

BEATON, CECIL – British portrait photographer, stage and costume designer for stage and film. Films include *My Fair Lady*.

BENNY, JACK – comedian, beginning in vaudeville, transitioning into radio, then television, adapting to each new medium and remaining a headliner throughout his life.

BERGHOF, HERBERT – co-founder with Uta Hagen of HB Studio in New York City.

BERGMAN, INGMAR – Swedish film auteur. *The Seventh Seal, Wild Strawberries, Persona, Cries and Whispers, Fanny and Alexander.*

BERTINELLI, VALERIE – television actress, *One Day at a Time, Touched by an Angel, Hot in Cleveland.*

BISHOP, ANDRE – Artistic Director of Lincoln Center Theater since 1992.

BLASS, BILL – American fashion designer, built a multi-million dollar fashion business bearing his name.

BOSWELL SISTERS – singing trio popular on radio and records in the 30s.

BRANTLEY, BEN – drama critic for *The New York Times.*

BREUER, MARCEL – Bauhaus architect, shaped 20th-century architecture. Designed Whitney Museum of American Art.

BROOKS, PATRICIA – lyric soprano who helped fashion the modern standard for opera performers.

BROWN, HELEN GURLEY – editor-in-chief of *Cosmopolitan* magazine for 32 years, author of *Sex and the Single Girl.*

BRUCE, LENNIE – 60s stand-up comedian, routines combined satire, politics, religion, sex. Resulting obscenity trial played key role in the Free Speech Movement.

BUCKLEY, BETTY – actress, singer, created the role of Grizabella in *Cats*. Film, *Frantic*.

BUCKLEY, PAT – socialite, wife of William F. Buckley, Jr. Leading player on Manhattan's social and charity benefit circuit.

BURNETT, CAROL – actress, first seen in the Broadway musical, *Once Upon a Mattress*, went on to star in *The Carol Burnett Show*.

BURTON, KATE – actress. Broadway, *Hedda Gabler, The Elephant Man*. Television, *Scandal*.

BUSCH, CHARLES – author and star of off-off Broadway plays: *Psycho Beach Party, Vampire Lesbians of Sodom*, and *Red Scare on Sunset*. Broadway author of *Tale of the Allergist's Wife*.

BUZZI, RUTH – comedienne featured on *Rowan & Martin's Laugh-In*.

CAGE, JOHN – 20th century composer, pioneer of avant-garde music.

CALLAS, MARIA – renowned opera singer, revived operas of Bellini, Donizetti, and Rossini.

CAPALBO, CARMEN – stage director, Broadway premiere of *A Moon for the Misbegotten* and historical revival of *The Three Penny Opera*.

CARLISLE, KITTY – actress, singer and arts advocate. Served as chairman of the New York Council on the Arts. Wife of Moss Hart.

CARROLL, LEWIS – British author, *Alice's Adventures in Wonderland, Through the Looking-Glass* (includes the poems, "Jabberwocky," "The Hunting of the Snark").

CARROLL, PAT – actress. Stage, *Gertrude Stein, Gertrude Stein, Gertrude Stein, The Merry Wives of Windsor* (Falstaff), Film, the voice of Ursula in *The Little Mermaid*.

CAVETT, DICK – former television talk show host. Landmark interviews: Groucho Marx, Katharine Hepburn and Marlon Brando.

CHANEL, COCO – legendary fashion designer and creator of fragrance *Chanel No. 5*.

CHANNING, CAROL – musical theater star, *Hello, Dolly* and *Gentlemen Prefer Blondes*.

CHARNIN, MARTIN – lyricist, writer and theater director. Director and lyricist of the musical *Annie*.

CHILD, JULIA – chef and star of the TV series *The French Chef*.

CHRISTIAN, LINDA – film actress, played Mara in the last Johnny Weissmuller Tarzan film, *Tarzan and the Mermaids*.

CHRISTOPHER, SYBIL – founded the 60s discotheque Arthur, The New Theater on 54th Street and The Bay Street Theater in Sag Harbor.

CIBELLI, RENATO – Broadway actor, singer. *Oklahoma, Happy Hunting, Milk and Honey, Man of La Mancha*.

CLIFT, MONTGOMERY – Hollywood star, *A Place in the Sun, I Confess, From Here to Eternity*.

CONNELL, GORDON – actor, composer, frequently performed with his wife, Jane. *Lysistrata* and *The Good Doctor.*

CONNELL, JANE – actress: Agnes Gooch in *Mame, New Faces of 1956* (introduced *April in Fairbanks.)*

COOK, BARBARA – actress, singer. Broadway musicals; *Plain and Fancy, Candide* and *The Music Man.* Concert career begun in 70s, continues.

COOPER, GARY – Hollywood star from the silent era through the golden age. *A Farewell to Arms, High Noon.*

COWARD, NOËL – English playwright, composer, actor. Plays, *Hay Fever, Private Lives, Design for Living, Present Laughter, Blithe Spirit.* Songs, *If Love Were All, I'll See You Again, A Room With a View, Mad Dogs and Englishmen, London Pride, I Went to a Marvelous Party.* Acting roles, *Private Lives, Tonight at 8:30.*

CRAWFORD, JOAN – Hollywood star, *Mildred Pierce, What Ever Happened to Baby Jane?*

CRYSTAL, BILLY – actor. Film, *When Harry Met Sally, City Slickers, Analyze This.* Stage, *700 Sundays.* Television, *Soap, Saturday Night Live,* Academy Awards host 9 times.

CULLUM, JOHN – actor, singer. Broadway, *On the Twentieth Century, Shenandoah, Show Boat.* Television, *Northern Exposure.*

CUMMING, ALAN – Scottish-American actor. Broadway, *Cabaret.* Television, *The Good Wife.*

CURIE, MADAME MARIE – French physicist, discovered radium and coined the term "radioactivity." First woman to win a Nobel Prize.

DANE, FAITH – actress, created the role of Mazeppa in *Gypsy*.

DABDOUB, JACK – actor in more than a dozen Broadway shows, including the original production of *Man of La Mancha*.

DA COSTA, MORTON "TEKE" – stage director, had the distinction of having four Broadway hits in three years during the mid-1950s, *Plain and Fancy*, *No Time for Sergeants*, *Auntie Mame* and *The Music Man*.

DAHL, ROALD – British writer, *Charlie and the Chocolate Factory*, *Matilda*.

DARLING, CANDY – actress, Warhol Superstar. *Flesh* and *Women in Revolt*.

DAVIS, BETTE – Hollywood star, *Of Human Bondage*, *Dark Victory*, *The Great Lie*, *Now Voyager*, *The Little Foxes*, *All About Eve*, *What Ever Happened to Baby Jane?*

DE HAVILLAND, OLIVIA – Hollywood star, *Snake Pit*, *The Heiress*, *Gone with the Wind*.

DELUISE, DOM – actor. Film, *The Twelve Chairs*, *Blazing Saddles*, *Silent Movie*, *History of the World, Part I*, *Spaceballs*, *Robin Hood: Men in Tights*, *Cannonball Run*, *The Best Little Whorehouse in Texas*. Television, *Candid Camera*, *The Dean Martin Show*.

DEPARDIEU, GÉRARD – French film star, *Get Our Your Handkerchiefs*, *Going Places*, *Green Card*, *Cyrano de Bergerac*.

DE PORTAGO, ALFONSO – Spanish racing driver.

DEPP, JOHNNY – Hollywood star, *Edward Scissorhands*, *Sleepy Hollow*, *Pirates of the Caribbean*.

DIETRICH, MARLENE – Hollywood star, singer, *The Blue Angel, Blonde Venus, Touch of Evil, Judgment at Nuremberg*. Later concert career in Las Vegas and Europe.

DISHY, BOB – actor. Stage, *Flora the Red Menace, The Price, Sly Fox, Grown Ups*. Film, *Lovers and Other Strangers, Brighton Beach*.

DOUGHERTY, MARION – casting director, cast some of Hollywood's biggest stars in their earliest parts.

DOUGLAS, KIRK – Hollywood star, *Spartacus, Lonely Are the Brave, Lust for Life, Gunfight at the O.K. Corral, The Bad and the Beautiful, The Vikings, Ace in the Hole, 20,000 Leagues Under the Sea*.

DOWLING, DORIS – actress in the film classics *The Lost Weekend, Blue Dahlia, Bitter Rice* and Orson Welles' *Othello*.

DOWNEY SR., ROBERT – actor and underground filmmaker, *Putney Swope, Greaser's Palace, Pound*.

DOVIMA – fashion model during the 1950s. Famous for the iconic Avedon photograph, "Dovima with the Elephants."

DRAPER, RUTH – actress, monologist, career spanned 40 years.

DUSE, ELEONORA – legendary actress. Early 20th century. Subject of Eva Le Gallienne book, *The Mystic in the Theater*, still in print today.

DUKAKIS, OLYMPIA – actress. Stage, *The Milk Train Doesn't Stop Here Anymore*. Film, *Moonstruck* (Oscar), *Steel Magnolias, Away from Her*.

DWIGHT, GEORGE – political activist and ardent gardener.

EBB, FRED – lyricist, half musical theater team of Kander and Ebb. Broadway musicals include *Cabaret* and *Chicago*.

EBERT, GABRIEL – actor, singer, originated roles in *4000 Miles*, *Matilda*, and *Robin Hood*.

ELIOT, T.S. – Nobel Prize-winning poet and playwright. Poems, "The Love Song of J. Alfred Prufrock," "The Wasteland." Plays, *The Hollow Men*, *Ash Wednesday*, *Murder in the Cathedral*.

EMERSON, FAYE – actress who achieved national popularity in the 1950s as one of television's first late-night interviewers.

EVANS, DAME EDITH – English stage star. Career spanned sixty years during which she played more than 100 roles.

FAIRBANKS, JR., DOUGLAS – actor, began in silent films.

FEINGOLD, MICHAEL – former drama critic for *The Village Voice*, now for TheaterMania.

FIELDS, W.C. – Hollywood star, *My Little Chickadee*, *Never Give a Sucker an Even Break*, *The Bank Dick*, *Poppy*, *David Copperfield*.

FISCHER-DIESKAU, DIETRICH – German lyric baritone and conductor of classical music, one of the most famous Lieder performers of the postwar period.

FISH, DANIEL – director of conceptually experimental stage productions, *True Love*, *The Black Monk*, *Paradise Park*, *Rocket to the Moon*.

FLEMING, RHONDA – 40s, 50s film actress, *The Big Circus*, *Gunfight at the O.K. Corral*.

FONTAINE, JOAN – Hollywood star, *Rebecca* (Oscar), *Suspicion*, *Jane Eyre*, *The Women*.

FRANKEL, SCOTT – musical theater composer in collaboration with lyricist Michael Korie, *Happiness, Grey Gardens, Meet Mr. Future, Doll, Far From Heaven*.

FRANKLIN, BONNIE – actress. Broadway, *Applause*. Television, *One Day at a Time*.

FREY, LEONARD – actor, theater and film. *Boys in the Band, Fiddler on the Roof*.

FROST, DAVID – journalist, television host, host of satirical news program, *That Was the Week That Was*.

FROST, ROBERT – American poet, "Stopping by the Woods on a Snowy Evening," "The Road Not Taken."

FURTH, GEORGE – playwright, actor, book for *Company* and the play *Twigs*. Film roles, *Butch Cassidy and the Sundance Kid, Blazing Saddles* and *Shampoo*.

GABLE, CLARK – Hollywood star, leading man over three decades. *Gone with the Wind, It Happened One Night, The Misfits*.

GARDNER, AVA – Hollywood star, *Mogambo, The Barefoot Contessa, The Night of the Iguana, Showboat*.

GATCHELL, R. TYLER – theatrical general manager and producer. With partner, Peter Neufeld served as executive producer of innumerable Broadway shows, including *Cats* and *Evita*.

GEFFEN, DAVID – business magnate, producer, film studio executive, and philanthropist.

GELDZAHLER, HENRY – art historian and curator, served as New York City Commissioner of Cultural Affairs.

GERSTEN, BERNARD – producer, driving force behind New York Shakespeare Festival and Lincoln Center Theater.

GHOSTLEY, ALICE – actress. Stage, *New Faces of 1952*, *The Beauty Part*, *A Thurber Carnival*. Film, *To Kill a Mockingbird*, *Grease*. Television, *Designing Women*, *Bewitched*, *Mayberry R.F.D.*

GILBERT, WILLIE – book writer with Jack Weinstock for the musicals *How to Succeed in Business Without Really Trying*, *Catch Me If You Can* and *Hot Spot*.

GODDARD, PAULETTE – Hollywood star of the 1930s, 40s and 50s. *Modern Times*, *The Great Dictator*, *The Women*.

GORDON, RUTH – Broadway actress for 50 years. Film, *Rosemary's Baby*, *Harold and Maude*, *Where's Poppa*. Screenwriter, *Adam's Rib*, *Pat and Mike*.

GOULD, HAROLD – stage, television actor, *Fools*, Jules Feiffer's *Grown Ups The Golden Girls*, *Rhoda*.

GRAHAM, RONNY – actor, *New Faces of 1952*, and screenwriter, *To Be Or Not To Be*, *Spaceballs*.

GREENE, ADOLPH – playwright, performer, lyricist, collaborator with Betty Comden on Broadway musicals, *On the Town*, *Wonderful Town*,

Bells Are Ringing, and screenplays, *Singin' in the Rain* and *The Band Wagon*.

GREIF, MICHAEL – stage director. Broadway musicals: *Rent, Grey Gardens, Next to Normal*.

GRIZZARD, GEORGE – actor, originated the roles of Nick in *Who's Afraid of Virginia Woolf?* and Tony in *The Royal Family; Delicate Balance* (Tony Award).

GUARE, JOHN – playwright, *The House of Blue Leaves, Six Degrees of Separation, Landscape of the Body*.

HAGEN, UTA – actress, teacher, author. Originated the role of Martha in *Who's Afraid of Virginia Woolf?* Co-founder with husband Herbert Berghof of HB Studios. Author, *Respect for Acting*.

HAMILTON, MARGARET – actress, Wicked Witch in *The Wizard of Oz*.

HAMLISCH, MARVIN – Broadway and film composer, *A Chorus Line, The Sting, The Way We Were*.

HARLEY, MARGOT – co-founder with John Houseman of *The Acting Company*.

HARPER, WALLY – Broadway musical arranger and composer. Composer, *Sensations*. Conductor/arranger for Barbara Cook.

HARRINGTON, JR., PAT – television actor, *One Day at a Time, The Steve Allen Show*.

HARRIS, BARBARA – actress, singer. Stage, *Oh Dad, Poor Dad, Mama's*

Hung You In The Closet and I'm Feelin' So Sad. Broadway, in musicals written for her, O*n a Clear Day You Can See Forever, The Apple Tree* (Tony). Film, *A Thousand Clowns, Nashville, Family Plot.*

HARRIS, JULIE – stage star, *Member of the Wedding, I Am a Camera, The Belle of Amherst, The Last of Mrs. Lincoln, Forty Carats.* Film, *Member of the Wedding, The Haunting, East of Eden.* 5 Tony Awards.

HARRIS, ROSEMARY – stage star, *The Lion in Winter (Tony), A Delicate Balance, Road to Mecca, The Royal Family, An Inspector Calls.* Film, *Before the Devil Knows You're Dead*, Aunt May in the three *Spider-Man* films.

HAWN, GOLDIE – Hollywood star, *Private Benjamin, The First Wives Club.* Television, *Rowan & Martin's Laugh-In.*

HAYES, HELEN – stage actress for 80 years, earned the title "First Lady of the American Theater."

HEAD, EDITH – Hollywood costume designer to the stars: Ginger Rogers, Bette Davis, Barbara Stanwyck, Shirley MacLaine and Grace Kelly. Films include *The Heiress* and *The Sting.*

HERZOG, AMY – playwright, *4000 Miles* (Pulitzer Prize finalist and Obie Award winner) *After the Revolution, The Great God Pan* and *Belleville.*

HEPBURN, AUDREY – Hollywood star, *Roman Holiday, Funny Face, My Fair Lady.*

HESTON, CHARLTON – Hollywood star, *The Ten Commandments, Ben Hur, El Cid, The Planet of the Apes.*

HIRSCHFELD, AL – artist, caricaturist, chronicling nearly all the major entertainment figures of the 20th century.

HOLLIDAY, JUDY – Stage and film star. Appeared in both stage and screen versions of *Born Yesterday* and *Bells Are Ringing*.

HORNE, LENA – actress, singer. Film, *Cabin in the Sky, Stormy Weather*. Stage, *Lena Horne: The Lady and Her Music*.

HUNTER, KIM – actress. Originated the role of Stella in *A Streetcar Named Desire*. Film, *A Streetcar Named Desire, Deadline USA, A Matter of Life and Death, Planet of the Apes*.

HUNTLEY, PAUL – master hair designer and wigmaker for stage and film. Honored in 2003 with a Lifetime Achievement Tony Award.

IRVING, GEORGE – actor in Broadway musicals, *Irene, Me and My Girl, So Long, 174th Street*. At age 86, performed one-man cabaret show at Feinstein's and received Hammerstein Award for Lifetime Achievement in Musical Theater.

ISHERWOOD, CHRISTOPHER – English novelist best known for the stories he wrote in the 1930s that served as the basis for the play, *I Am a Camera* and the musical *Cabaret*.

IVES, CHARLES – composer, employed experimental techniques that foreshadowed musical innovations.

JAGGER, MICK – lead vocalist of The Rolling Stones.

JONSON, BEN – 17th century English writer of satirical plays, *Every Man in His Humour, Volpone, The Alchemist*.

JORDAN, RICHARD – stage, screen and television actor. Member of the New York Shakespeare Festival.

KANDER, JOHN – composer, half musical theater team of Kander and Ebb. Broadway musicals include *Cabaret* and *Chicago*.

KANIN, GARSON – writer and director. Authored *Born Yesterday*, and with wife Ruth Gordon co-authored Tracy-Hepburn movies. Directed *The Diary of Anne Frank* and *Funny Girl*.

KAVNER, JULIE – television actress, voice-over artist, *The Simpsons*, *Rhoda*.

KEATON, BUSTER – silent film star. Films, *The General*, *The Navigator*.

KENNEDY, ROSE – matriarch of the Kennedy political dynasty, mother of President John F. Kennedy.

KERT, LARRY – actor, singer, and dancer. Originated the role of Tony in *West Side Story*.

KILGALLEN, DOROTHY – newspaper columnist, covered gossip, entertainment and politics.

KING, ALAN – comedian, actor, developed from borscht-belt comic to social satirist. Films, *Casino*, *Just Tell Me What You Want*.

KING, CAROLE – songwriter, singer, with husband and lyricist Gerry Goffin: "Will You Love Me Tomorrow," "Natural Woman," "So Far Away," "I Feel the Earth Move," and "You've Got a Friend."

KIRBY, BRUCE – television actor, *Goodyear Television Playhouse*, *Columbo*, *The Sopranos*.

KLEIN, ROBERT – stand-up comic, actor. Television, eight live HBO specials 1975 – 2005. Film, *Hooper, Primary Colors, Reign Over Me.*

KORIE, MICHAEL – musical theater lyricist, in collaboration with composer Scott Frankel, *Happiness, Grey Gardens, Meet Mr. Future, Doll, Far From Heaven.*

KRASS, MICHAEL – Broadway costume designer. *Machinal, The Constant Wife, You're a Good Man Charlie Brown, After the Fall, Twelve Angry Men.*

LADD, ALAN – Hollywood star of 40s and 50s noir and westerns. *Shane, The Blue Dahlia.*

LAHR, BERT – Broadway star, *Foxy, The Beauty Part, Waiting for Godot.* Film, *The Wizard of Oz.*

LAMOS, MARK – theater, opera director, producer, actor. Film, *Longtime Companion.* Artistic Director of the Westport Country Playhouse.

LANE, KENNETH JAY – costume jewelry designer, created designs for Jacqueline Onassis, Elizabeth Taylor, Diana Vreeland, and Audrey Hepburn.

LANSBURY, ANGELA – Star for 70 years. Film, *Gaslight, Manchurian Candidate.* Broadway, *Mame, Sweeney Todd, Gypsy, Blithe Spirit.* Television, *Murder, She Wrote.*

LANZA, MARIO – American tenor, movie star of 40s and 50s.

LAURENTS, ARTHUR – playwright, director, screenwriter. Broadway, book for *Gypsy, West Side Story.* Directed revivals of both. Screenplays, *The Way We Were, The Turning Point.*

LAZAR, IRVING "SWIFTY" – talent agent and dealmaker of the golden age of Broadway and Hollywood. Represented performers, writers and producers.

LEE, GYPSY ROSE – entertainer in vaudeville and burlesque whose memoir was the basis for the musical *Gypsy*.

LEAR, NORMAN – television producer, writer, creator of sitcoms *All in the Family, Maude, The Jeffersons, Sanford & Son, One Day at a Time, Good Times*, and *Mary Hartman, Mary Hartman.*

LEE, PEGGY – singer, jazz and pop. Hits include: *Fever, Is That All There Is?*

LE GALLIENNE, EVA – Broadway star for 70 years. *The Royal Family, Mary Stuart, To Grandmother's House We Go, Alice in Wonderland.*

LENYA, LOTTE – German actress. Stage, *The Threepenny Opera, Cabaret.* Film, *From Russia With Love, The Roman Spring of Mrs. Stone.*

LEVENE, SAM – stage and film actor for 50 years. Originated roles in 33 Broadway productions, *Three Men on A Horse, Dinner at Eight, Room Service, Light Up the Sky, Heartbreak House, The Sunshine Boys, Guys and Dolls.* Films, *Three Men on a Horse, The Babe Ruth Story, Sweet Smell of Success.*

LIBERTINI, RICHARD – actor, original cast member of *The Mad Show.* Films, *Don't Drink the Water, Days of Heaven, Popeye.*

LILLIE, BEATRICE – British comedienne, muse to Noel Coward and Cole Porter. Broadway, *High Spirits.* Film, *Thoroughly Modern Millie.* Earned title "the funniest woman in the world."

LINDBERGH, CHARLES – the first man to fly the Atlantic solo nonstop.

LOQUASTO, SANTO – set and costume designer. Dance, *Don Quixote*. Stage, *Bullets Over Broadway, A Delicate Balance, Wit*. Film, *Bullets Over Broadway, Radio Days, Zelig*.

LORAYNE, HARRY – magician, memory-training specialist and writer. Called "The Yoda of Memory Training" by *Time* magazine.

LORTEL, LUCILLE – producer, owned and operated the Theatre de Lys, later renamed the Lucille Lortel.

LOUDON, DOROTHY – Broadway actress and singer, winner of the Tony Award for her performance as Miss Hannigan in *Annie*.

LOY, MYRNA – Hollywood star, Nora Charles in *The Thin Man* series, *Mr. Blandings Builds His Dream House, Cheaper By the Dozen, The Bachelor and the Bobby-Soxer, Lonelyhearts, Midnight Lace, Just Tell Me What You Want*.

LUCKINBILL, LAURENCE – actor, stage and film. Plays, *Poor Murderer, A Prayer for My Daughter*. Films, *Star Trek V: The Final Frontier*.

LUPONE, PATTI – Broadway and London musical star. Original productions of *Evita, Les Misérables, Sunset Boulevard*. Tony winner for revival of *Gypsy*.

MAHER, JOE – actor. Stage, *Loot, The Prime of Miss Jean Brodie, King Henry V, The Royal Family*, and *Night and Day*. Film, *Heaven Can Wait, Sister Act*.

MANN, TED – producer, director, co-founder with Jose Quintero of Circle in the Square Theater.

MARSH, JEAN – British actress, writer, co-created and starred in the TV series *Upstairs, Downstairs*, co-created the television series *The House of Eliott.*

MARSHALL, MORT – Uncle Jocko in the original *Gypsy*. Films, *Kiss Me Deadly, The Longest Yard.*

MARTIN, NICHOLAS – stage director, *Full Gallop, Betty's Summer Vacation, Hedda Gabler, Vanya and Sonia and Masha and Spike.*

MARX, GROUCHO – Hollywood and television star. Film, *Monkey Business, Duck Soup, Horse Feathers, A Night at the Opera, A Day at the Races.* Television, *You Bet Your Life.*

MAXWELL, ELSA – professional hostess from the 20s through the 50s, mingling royalty, high society and movie stars.

MAY, ELAINE – actress, screenwriter, director. Wrote, directed and starred in *A New Leaf*. Screenplays, *Ishtar, Heaven Can Wait, Primary Colors, Birdcage.*

MAZOR, BOAZ – fashion presence, sales director for Oscar de la Renta.

MACGRAW, ALI – actress, achieved sudden stardom in the film *Love Story.*

MEADOW, LYNNE – producer, director. Artistic director of The Manhattan Theater club.

MEISNER, SANFORD – actor and acting coach, long associated with the Neighborhood Playhouse.

MENDES, SAM – director, theater and film. Stage, revivals of *Cabaret, Oliver, Company, Gypsy*. Film, *American Beauty, Road to Perdition, Skyfall*.

MENGERS, SUE – agent, shaped Hollywood moviemaking in the 1970's.

MERCER, MABEL – British-born singer, star of Manhattan cabaret for 40 years, influenced stylings of Billie Holiday, Nat King Cole, Johnny Mathis, Barbara Cook, Bobby Short, Frank Sinatra.

MERMAN, ETHEL – musical comedy legend, *Girl Crazy, Anything Goes, DuBarry Was a Lady, Happy Hunting, Call Me Madam, Annie Get Your Gun, Gypsy*.

MYERS, MIKE – actor, screenwriter. Television, *Saturday Night Live*. Film, *Wayne's World, Austin Powers: International Man of Mystery*, voice of *Shrek*.

MILLER, ANN – Hollywood star of MGM musicals, *Easter Parade, On the Town*, and *Kiss Me Kate*. Later on Broadway with Mickey Rooney in *Sugar Babies*.

MILLER, ARTHUR – playwright and screenwriter. Stage, *All My Sons, Death of a Salesman, The Crucible*, and *A View from the Bridge*. Film, *The Misfits*.

MILLER, ROGER – singer, songwriter, Broadway and pop. Hits include *King of the Road*. Theater, composer/lyricist/actor, *Big River*.

MINNELLI, LIZA – Hollywood, television and concert star. Film, *Cabaret* (Oscar), *Arthur, New York, New York, The Sterile Cuckoo*. Television, *Liza With a Z*. Concert, Carnegie Hall, Radio City Music Hall.

MINOR, PHILIP – actor, director, specializing in Shaw Plays. Sheridan Square Playhouse, Circle in the Square Theater.

MIRABELLA, GRACE – former editor-in-chief of *Vogue*, replaced Diana Vreeland. Subsequently founded *Mirabella* magazine.

MITCHELL, JONI – singer, songwriter. Hits include: *Both Sides Now, Chelsea Morning, Big Yellow Taxi and Woodstock.*

MONK, JULIUS – impresario of the New York cabaret scene, created satiric revues in a series of supper clubs: the Ruban Bleu in the early 1940s, the Downstairs, the Upstairs at the Downstairs and, in the late 1960s, Plaza 9 at the Plaza Hotel.

MONT, IRA – stage manager of over 15 Broadway shows, including *The Producers, Young Frankenstein, A Little Night Music, The Norman Conquests, Cinderella.*

MOORE, GARY – pioneer in early television, introduced Carol Burnett, Don Knotts, Alan King and Jonathan Winters.

MORENO, RITA – actress, singer, stage, film and television. *Last of the Red Hot Lovers, The Ritz, The Odd Couple, West Side Story, Carnal Knowledge, Oz.*

MORSE, ROBERT – actor, star of both original Broadway production and movie version of *How to Succeed in Business Without Really Trying* and the one-man show *Tru.* Television, *Mad Men.*

MULLIGAN, GERRY – musician, baritone saxophonist. With trumpeter Chet Baker, credited with creating the Cool School of jazz.

NABORS, JIM – television actor, Gomer Pyle on *The Andy Griffith Show* and the spin-off *Gomer Pyle, U.S.M.C.*

NEAL, PATRICIA – Hollywood star, *Hud, The Fountainhead, The Subject Was Roses, A Face in the Crowd, In Harm's Way.*

NEDERLANDER, AMY – Broadway producer, *The Diary of Anne Frank, Salome, Whoopi, Democracy, Thurgood, The Merchant of Venice.*

NICHOLS, MIKE – director, producer. Film, *The Graduate, Who's Afraid of Virginia Woolf?, Catch-22, Silkwood, Working Girl, The Birdcage.* Television, *Wit, Angels in America.* Stage, *Spamalot, Death of a Salesman,* for which he accepted a Tony Award at age 80.

NICHOLSON, JACK – Hollywood star, *Easy Rider, Five Easy Pieces, One Flew Over the Cuckoo's Nest, Chinatown, The Shining, Reds, A Few Good Men, Terms of Endearment, Prizzi's Honor, About Schmidt, The Departed.*

NOONE, JAMES – set designer, *Frankie and Johnny in the Clair de Lune, Three Tall Women, Full Gallop, Fully Committed, Jekyll & Hyde, A Class Act.*

NYKVIST, SVEN – Swedish cinematographer, associated with Ingmar Bergman, winning Academy Awards for work on two Bergman films, *Cries and Whispers, Fanny and Alexander.*

O'BRIEN, JACK – Broadway director, producer. Musicals, *Damn Yankees, The Full Monty, Hairspray.* Plays, *The Piano Lesson, The Coast of Utopia, Hamlet.* Opera, *Il Trittico* at the Metropolitan Opera. Three Tony Awards.

O'HARE, DENIS – actor. Stage, *Cabaret, Take Me Out, Sweet Charity, An Iliad.* Film, *Charlie Wilson's War, Milk, Changeling, The Dallas Buyers Club.* Television, *True Blood, American Horror Story.*

OLDMAN, GARY – film actor, *Sid and Nancy, Prick Up Your Ears, JFK, Bram Stoker's Dracula, Harry Potter* series, *Dark Knight* trilogy, *Dawn of the Planet of the Apes.*

OLIVIER, SIR LAURENCE – English stage and film star. Stage, original *Private Lives.* Film, *Henry V, Wuthering Heights, Rebecca, The Entertainer, Marathon Man.*

ONASSIS, JACQUELINE KENNEDY – widow of President John F. Kennedy. Subsequently a book editor. Instrumental in saving Grand Central Terminal from demolition.

OSMOND, DONNY – singer, teamed with sister in the TV variety show *Donny & Marie.*

PAGE, GERALDINE – stage and film star. Stage, *Summer and Smoke, Clothes for a Summer Hotel, Agnes of God.* Film, *The Trip to Bountiful* (Oscar), *Sweet Bird of Youth.*

PAPP, JOSEPH – producer, founder of The New York Shakespeare Festival and The Public Theater.

PARKER, DOROTHY – poet, short story writer, satirist associated with *The New Yorker* and the Algonquin Round Table.

PARKER, GILBERT – literary agent, represented major American playwrights.

PARKER, SUZY – the first supermodel. Active from 1947 into the early 1960s, first to earn $100,000 a year.

PATCHETT, JEAN – fashion model, 1940s through 60s. Credited with introducing the image of the remote, unattainable woman in fashion advertising.

PECK, GREGORY – Hollywood star of the 50s and 60s. *To Kill A Mockingbird* (Oscar), *Gentleman's Agreement, Twelve O'Clock High*.

PENN, SEAN – actor. Films, *Dead Man Walking, Mystic River* (Oscar), *Milk* (Oscar).

PERELMAN, S.J. – writer, humorist primarily associated with *The New Yorker*. Also stage *The Beauty Part* and film *Around The World in 80 Days* and Marx Brothers movies, *Horse Feathers, Monkey Business*.

PHILLIPS, MACKENZIE – actress, film and television, *American Graffiti, One Day at a Time*.

PIAZZOLLA, ASTOR – Argentine tango composer, created "nuevo tango" incorporating elements of jazz and classical into traditional tango music.

PLIMPTON, GEORGE – journalist, writer, literary editor, founder of the *Paris Review*.

PORCELLI, CARMINE – fashion executive, best known in the industry as Director of Licensing for Esprit in New York City.

PORTER, COLE – legendary composer, Broadway musicals, *Anything Goes, Kiss Me Kate, High Society, Can-Can*.

POWELL, LOVELADY – film actress, *I Never Sang for My Father, The Happy Hooker, The Possession of Joel Delaney*.

PRINCE, HAL – Broadway producer and director, *Company, Follies, A Little Night Music, Sweeney Todd, Evita, Fiddler on the Roof, Kiss of the Spider Woman, Cabaret, Show Boat, Phantom of the Opera* (now running on Broadway for over 25 years.)

PRYCE, JONATHAN – actor. Broadway, *Comedians* (Tony Award), *Miss Saigon* (Tony Award). Film, *Carrington, Brazil, Evita, Glengarry Glen Ross, Tomorrow Never Dies, Pirates of the Caribbean.*

QUINTERO, JOSE – director, founder of Circle in the Square Theater. Plays, *Summer and Smoke, Our Town, The Iceman Cometh. Broadway,* premiere production of *Long Day's Journey Into Night.* Film, *The Roman Spring of Mrs. Stone.*

RABB, ELLIS – actor, director. *You Can't Take it With You, The Royal Family, The Philadelphia Story, A Life in the Theater.*

RAITT, JOHN – actor singer, originated roles in *Carousel* and *The Pajama Gam*e.

RAYNER, CHESSY – decorator, founder of design company with partner Mica Ertegun.

REDGRAVE, LYNN – actress. Stage, *Black Comedy/White Lies, My Fat Friend, Shakespeare for My Father.* Film, *Georgy Girl, Gods and Monsters.*

REED, PAMELA – actress. Stage, *Getting Out* (Obie). Film, *The Right Stuff, The Best of Times, Kindergarten Cop.* Television, *Parks and Recreation.*

REEVE, CHRISTOPHER – stage and film actor, activist. Broadway, *The Fifth of July, A Matter of Gravity.* Film, *Superman, Death Trap.* Founder, Christopher Reeve Foundation.

REVSON, CHARLES – businessman, philanthropist, founder of the cosmetics company, Revlon.

REYNOLDS, BURT – Hollywood and television star. Film, *Deliverance, Smokey and the Bandit, White Lightning, The Longest Yard, Boogie Nights (Golden Globe)*. Television, *Evening Shade* (Emmy).

REYNOLDS, DEBBIE – Hollywood musical star, *Singin' in the Rain, The Unsinkable Molly Brown*. Later starred on Broadway in *Irene*.

RIFKIN, RON – actor. Stage, *Substance of Fire, Three Hotels, Cabaret* (Tony). Film, *Manhattan Murder Mystery, L.A. Confidential*. Television, *Alias, Brothers and Sisters*.

RIVERS, JOAN – stand-up comic, writer, television personality.

ROBARDS, JR., JASON – actor. Stage, *The Iceman Cometh, A Moon for the Misbegotten, Long Day's Journey Into Night*. Film, *A Thousand Clowns, Julia, All the President's Men, Magnolia*.

ROBBINS, JEROME – director, choreographer New York City Ballet, Broadway. *On the Town, Peter Pan, The King and I, West Side Story, Gypsy* and *Fiddler on the Roof*. Film, *West Side Story*.

ROBBINS, REX – Broadway and film actor, *Gypsy* with Angela Lansbury, *Richard III* with Al Pacino, S*isters Rosensweig*. Film, *The Royal Tenenbaums, 1776, Shaft*.

RODGERS, MARY – Broadway composer, *Once Upon a Mattress, Hot Spot*. Novelist, *Freaky Friday*.

RODGERS, RICHARD – composer, first with Lorenz Hart, then Oscar Hammerstein, *Pal Joey, The King and I, Oklahoma, Carousel, South Pacific, Flower Drum Song, The Sound of Music*.

ROGERS, GINGER – Hollywood star, Fred Astaire's dancing partner in a series of ten Hollywood musicals.

ROSENBLUM, EDGAR – executive director Long Wharf Theater. Premiered *The Gin Game, The Shadow Box, The Changing Room.*

ROSS, HERBERT – Broadway choreographer, film director. Choreographed *I Can Get It for You Wholesale.* Directed films *A Turning Point, Footloose, Steel Magnolias, The Sunshine Boys.*

ROWAN & MARTIN – comedy duo, hosts of the sketch comedy show *Laugh-In.* Introduced Lily Tomlin and Goldie Hawn, Ruth Buzzi, Jo Anne Worley and Alan Sues.

RUBINSTEIN, HELENA – cosmetics magnate, founder of Helena Rubinstein Incorporated.

RYAN, D.D. – editor at *Harper's Bazaar* under Diana Vreeland, costume designer for Broadway, *Company.*

SAKS, GENE – actor, stage, film director. Broadway, *Biloxi Blues, Brighton Beach Memoirs, Lost in Yonkers, Broadway Bound, The Odd Couple, California Suite.* Film, *Barefoot in the Park, The Odd Couple, Cactus Flower, Mame.*

SALINGER, J.D. – author, *The Catcher in the Rye, Nine Stories, Franny and Zooey,* and *Raise High the Roof Beam, Carpenters and Seymour: An Introduction.*

SANFORD, TIM – Artistic Director of Playwright's Horizons Theater since 1996.

SEGAL, DAVID – lighting designer for over 15 Broadway productions, including *Oh, Calcutta, Irene* and *Damn Yankees.*

SEGAL, GEORGE – actor. Film, *Ship of Fools, Who's Afraid of Virginia Woolf?, Blume in Love, Where's Poppa?* Television, *Just Shoot Me, Entourage, The Goldbergs.*

SHALHOUB, TONY – actor. Broadway, *Lend Me a Tenor, Golden Boy, Act One.* Television, *Monk* (three Emmys, Golden Globe).

SHAW, ARTIE – musician, led popular big bands in the late 30s and 40s.

SHEVELOVE, BURT – playwright, lyricist, librettist, director. *A Funny Thing Happened on the Way to the Forum, No, No, Nanette.*

SIMON, DANNY – TV writer, *Your Show of Shows, The Carol Burnett Show, The Facts of Life.*

SIMON, NEIL – playwright, wrote a series Broadway successes over a period of 40 years. Awarded Pulitzer Prize for *Lost in Yonkers.*

SMITH, ALEXIS – actress in 40s films opposite Errol Flynn, Frederic March, Cary Grant. Broadway, *Follies.*

SONDHEIM, STEPHEN – Broadway composer/lyricist, *A Funny Thing Happened on the Way to the Forum, Company, Follies, A Little Night Music, Sweeney Todd, Sunday in the Park with George, Into the Woods.* Lyricist, *West Side Story, Gypsy.*

SPENDER, STEPHEN – British poet, critic and novelist.

STANLEY, KIM – stage star, *Bus Stop, Picnic.* Film, *The Goddess, Séance on a Wet Afternoon, Frances.*

STAPLETON, MAUREEN – stage star, *The Rose Tattoo, Little Foxes, Orpheus Descending, The Gingerbread Lady, The Country Girl.* Film, *Reds, Interiors.* (Oscar, Emmy, two Tonys, British Academy Award.)

STEVENS, ROGER – Founding Chairman of The Kennedy Center. Instrumental in creation of National Endowment for the Arts.

STREEP, MERYL – stage and film star, winning Oscars for *Kramer vs. Kramer, Sophie's Choice, The Iron Lady.* Other films: *Ironweed, The Devil Wears Prada, Postcards from the Edge, Silkwood.*

STREISAND, BARBRA – mega-star of stage, film, recording.

STRITCH, ELAINE – Broadway actress, singer, original productions of *Bus Stop, Sail Away, Company;* revival, *A Delicate Balance* and one-woman show, *Elaine Stritch at Liberty.*

STRUTHERS, SALLY – actress, Archie Bunker's daughter on *All in the Family.*

STONE, DAVID – Broadway producer, *Wicked. If/Then, Next to Normal, The 25th Annual Putnam County Spelling Bee.*

STYNE, JULE – prolific composer "Just In Time," "Let It Snow," "I'll Walk Alone," "I Fall In Love Too Easily," "I've Heard That Song Before." Broadway shows: *Gentlemen Prefer Blondes, Bells Art Ringing, Do Re Mi, Funny Girl.*

THOMPSON, EMMA – actress, screenwriter. Academy Award for screenplay, *Sense and Sensibility.* Film roles: *The Remains of the Day, In the Name of the Father, Sense and Sensibility.* Television: *Wit, Angels in America.*

THORNDIKE, DAME SYBIL – British stage actress, originated title role in *St. Joan*, written for her by George Bernard Shaw.

TILLSTROM, BURR – puppeteer and creator of the television series *Kukla, Fran and Ollie*.

TOMLIN, LILY – actress. Television, *Rowan & Martin's Laugh-In*. Films, *Nashville, Nine to Five, Big Business*. Stage, *The Search for Signs of Intelligent Life in the Universe*.

TWITTY, CONWAY – country singer, often partnered with Loretta Lynn.

VICIOUS, SID – English guitarist and vocalist, the *Sex Pistols*.

VREELAND, ALEXANDER – founder of IFF International Flavors and Fragrances, creating and marketing Diana Vreeland Parfums, grandson of Diana Vreeland.

VREELAND, FREDERICK "FRECKIE" – diplomat, writer, son of Diana Vreeland. Served as Ambassador to Morocco.

VREELAND, NICHOLAS – ordained Tibetan monk, grandson of Diana Vreeland.

VREELAND, REED – banker, husband of Diana Vreeland.

VREELAND, TIMOTHY – architect, son of Diana Vreeland.

VUILLARD, JEAN-EDOUARD – French painter and printmaker.

WAITS, TOM – singer-songwriter, composer, and actor. Films, *Paradise Alley, Bram Stoker's Dracula, Down by Law*.

WALKER, NANCY – actress. Broadway, original productions of *On the Town, Pal Joey, Wonderful Town, Do Re Mi*. Television, *Mary Tyler Moore Show, Rhoda*.

WALLOWITCH, JOHN – cabaret singer and prolific songwriter, fixture of the New York cabaret world for more than 40 years.

WARHOL, ANDY – pop art artist, filmmaker, founded *Interview* magazine.

WELLES, ORSON – film auteur. *Citizen Kane, The Magnificent Ambersons, Touch of Evil, Macbeth, Othello, The Lady from Shanghai, The Trial*.

WEINSTOCK, JACK – playwright, *How to Succeed in Business Without Really Trying, Catch Me If You Can, Hot Spot*.

WEISSLER, FRAN & BARRY – husband-and-wife producing team. Revivals of *Chicago, Annie Get Your Gun, La Cage aux Folles*.

WEYMOUTH, LALLY – American journalist, Senior Associate Editor of the *Washington Post*.

WIDDOES, KATHLEEN – stage, film, television actress, N.Y. Shakespeare Festival star. *Much Ado About Nothing, Franny's Way* (Lortel Award). Films, *The Group, The Seagull, Savages*.

WILDER, BILLY – filmmaker, screenwriter, producer. Career spanned more than 50 years and 60 films, *The Seven Year Itch, Double Indemnity, The Lost Weekend, Sunset Boulevard, Some Like It Hot, The Apartment*.

WILDER, THORNTON – playwright and novelist, winner of three Pulitzer Prizes – one for the novel, *The Bridge of San Luis Rey*, two for plays, *Our Town, The Skin of Our Teeth*.

WILLIAMS, ESTHER – swimming actress, star of MGM "aquamusicals."

WILLIAMS, TENNESSEE – playwright, *The Glass Menagerie, A Streetcar Named Desire, Cat on a Hot Tin Roof.*

WILSON, ELIZABETH – actress, stage and film. Stage, *Picnic, Sticks and Bones (Tony), Threepenny Opera, Morning's at Seven* and *A Delicate Balance.* Film, *The Goddess, The Birds, The Graduate, Catch-22, Nine to Five, Addams Family, Quiz Show.*

WINDSOR, DUKE AND DUCHESS OF – former King of England, abdicated throne to marry American divorcée.

WRAY, FAY – film actress, *King Kong.*

WRIGHT, DOUG – playwright, *I Am My Own Wife* (Pulitzer Prize), *Grey Gardens, The Little Mermaid, Hands on a Hard Body, Quills* (play and film).

THANK YOU

Thanks to John Bowers, Mark Hampton, Vangeli Kaseluris, Susan Krawitz, Duncan Maginnis, Dennis McCarthy, Ron Nyswaner, John Seidman, Laura Shaine, Nina Shengold, Zack Sklar, Mark St. Germain, and Carl Walker.